"YOU'RE RUINING MY LIFE!"

"YOU'RE RUINING MY LIFE!"

(But Not Really)

SURVIVING THE TEENAGE YEARS WITH
CONNECTED PARENTING

JENNIFER KOLARI MSW, RSW

VIKING
CANADA

VIKING CANADA

Published by the Penguin Group

Penguin Group (Canada), 90 Eglinton Avenue East, Suite 700,
Toronto, Ontario, Canada M4P 2Y3 (a division of Pearson Canada Inc.)

Penguin Group (USA) Inc., 375 Hudson Street, New York, New York 10014, U.S.A.
Penguin Books Ltd, 80 Strand, London WC2R 0RL, England
Penguin Ireland, 25 St Stephen's Green, Dublin 2, Ireland
(a division of Penguin Books Ltd)
Penguin Group (Australia), 250 Camberwell Road, Camberwell, Victoria 3124, Australia
(a division of Pearson Australia Group Pty Ltd)
Penguin Books India Pvt Ltd, 11 Community Centre, Panchsheel Park,
New Delhi – 110 017, India
Penguin Group (NZ), 67 Apollo Drive, Rosedale, Auckland 0632, New Zealand
(a division of Pearson New Zealand Ltd)
Penguin Books (South Africa) (Pty) Ltd, 24 Sturdee Avenue, Rosebank,
Johannesburg 2196, South Africa

Penguin Books Ltd, Registered Offices: 80 Strand, London WC2R 0RL, England

First published 2011

1 2 3 4 5 6 7 8 9 10   (RRD)

Copyright © Jennifer Kolari, 2011

Manufactured in the U.S.A.

LIBRARY AND ARCHIVES CANADA CATALOGUING IN PUBLICATION

Kolari, Jennifer
"You're ruining my life!" (but not really) : surviving the teenage years with connected
parenting / Jennifer Kolari.

Includes bibliographical references and index.
ISBN 978-0-670-06842-5

1. Parent and teenager. 2. Adolescent psychology.
3. Parenting—Psychological aspects. I. Title.

HQ799.15.K65 2011   649'.125   C2011-903215-5

Visit the Penguin Group (Canada) website at **www.penguin.ca**

Special and corporate bulk purchase rates available; please see
www.penguin.ca/corporatesales or call 1-800-810-3104, ext. 2477 or 2474

For Mom and Dad

Contents

Your Amazing Crazy Teen

What if I told you there's a medication you could administer to your teens that would help regulate their moods, increase their sense of trust, and improve their overall brain function? And that it's free, has no negative side effects, and helps boost the immune system? Now, what if I also told you that you already possess this medication in endless supply?

You'd probably say, "No way. Nothing can do all that, and if it could, everyone would know about it." But nurturing, compassion, and deep understanding *can* do all that and more, releasing reward chemicals that not only stimulate positive emotions but also increase order and balance in the nervous system. These chemicals, which include natural opiates, endorphins, and a powerful hormone called oxytocin, reduce and inhibit the stress hormone cortisol and bathe the brain in positive emotions that ripple through every cell in the body. Physician Gabor Maté put it beautifully: "Love is the drug kids need."

I don't mean to go all flower-power on you and don't expect you to hold hands and sing "Kumbaya," but the benefits of empathy and compassion have a strong basis in science that cannot be underestimated. Think of nurturing, compassion, and deep understanding as brain food, the emotional nutrition that we all need and that our teenagers may need most of all.

Parenting a teen can be amazing and wonderful, but it can also be confusing and overwhelming. Trying to reason with a fourteen-year-old is extraordinarily frustrating, and trying to do so in the midst of a wild "I love you, I hate you. I need you ... Go away, you're ruining my life" push/pull dance can seem downright impossible. Navigating through the major mood swings, the boundary-pushing, the door-slamming, and the arguments over every little thing can be an exhausting whirlwind that in your worst moments will leave you wondering why on earth you ever had kids at all (and then feeling guilty for having had that thought).

Connected Parenting, the therapeutic model I created and use with my clients, is a two-step program of empathy followed by guidance. This is a system based on the understanding that correcting and guiding behavior cannot and will not work unless preceded by and linked to empathy—the ability to identify with and have a deep understanding of the feelings of another person. Empathy is always an important component of parenting, but it's essential when you're dealing with adolescents, because it allows you to connect with them on an emotional level at a time when the thinking part of their brain is not yet fully developed. Until your teen "feels" your love and understanding, he won't be able to hear anything else you have to say.

A lot has been written about teens being sullen, noncommunicative, insolent, rebellious, and all kinds of other not-very-flattering adjectives. I'm sure you've used one or more of these terms yourself when describing your worst moments with your teenager. (You may even remember your parents describing you that way.) And teens certainly can be difficult. They often take things personally, fly off the handle, and experience powerful surges of emotions they don't understand. Social pressures and peer relationships pull on the parent–child bond, resulting in hurt feelings and an impossible tug-of-war between home and the outside world. But inside that sullen, rebellious kid you've sometimes got living under your roof there's a wonderful person waiting to get out. In fact, the average teenager's capacity to be silent and sulky one minute and sensitive, affectionate, and intelligent the next is positively astonishing.

Many people come to me grieving the loss of the sweet little girl or the rambunctious, adorable little boy who has, as far as they can tell, mysteriously disappeared and been replaced by an alien or an evil twin who no longer wants to be seen with them in public. If that's how you feel you're not alone, but you need to know that your child has not been abducted by extraterrestrials. He is simply experiencing one of the most intense and complicated transitions of his entire life. His body—and more importantly—his brain are undergoing enormous changes as he moves from childhood to adulthood. You probably just wish he'd let you help him through it instead of treating you as the enemy.

Well, the facts are these: you're not going to get your toddler back (would you really want to go through all that again anyway?), but you can get your child back—bigger, better, and bonded to you on a whole new level. One of the greatest pleasures you can have is watching your child turn into an adult with opinions, political beliefs, ideas, and dreams. You may find yourself enjoying his sense of humor, having meaningful conversations, and, in general, relating to this burgeoning adult in completely unexpected ways.

At the heart of Connected Parenting is the CALM (Connect, Affect, Listen, Mirror) technique. In Chapter Three I'll provide a full explanation of how it works and how you can use it with your teen. Although its principles are easy to understand, practicing it properly can be tough. It takes commitment and a willingness to try whenever possible to be non-defensive and to choose your words carefully. The rewards are well worth the effort and will last a lifetime.

The CALM technique will enhance all the other parenting techniques you may already use and all the knowledge you may already have. There are many fine books about parenting teens, many of which talk about why it's so important to listen to your teen and to be empathic. What few books tell you, however, is *how* to be empathic and, most importantly, how to move beyond empathy to manage and correct difficult, dangerous, or unacceptable behaviors. The whole point of the CALM technique is to empathize not only so that your teen will feel safe and understood but also so that you, the parent, will be better able to positively affect and guide his behavior. It's a beautiful gift to your teen and a lovely way to parent.

Many of us think we're empathic, but as easy as it sounds, being empathic and listening well are difficult skills. To master them requires patience and thoughtfulness. It is essential to adopt a neutral stance when issues arise, and that neutrality can be extremely difficult to maintain when you're hurt or angered by something your teen has done. What's more, empathy in itself isn't enough. We also need to know what to do next. My method takes you a step farther and provides a blueprint for creating positive change. The skills I teach may sometimes seem counterintuitive, but you can acquire them, just as my clients do, with the help and support I'm going to provide. In the beginning you may have to trust that what you're doing will work, but when it does, it will be life-altering for both you and your teen.

While I'm sure you believe that your child knows you love him and that whatever you have to say to him is for his own good, it isn't that simple. Adolescents are conflicted: they need and want your guidance at the same time that they're pulling away and establishing their independence. As a result they can be unpredictable and often not-so-nice. The attachment between you can fray, leaving them wondering not simply whether they're loved but whether they're lovable.

And parents may find it difficult to reassure their teens when they can be so nasty, hurtful, and cruel. Because we love them and do so much for them, what we perceive as their rejection or dismissal is both painful and provoking. It's normal and natural to pull away from and defend ourselves against someone who makes us feel so awful, even if it's our own child. And when we do become resentful, withdraw, or demand respect, the situation often becomes worse instead of better, leaving us even more baffled and frustrated.

Many of my clients have admitted that they find themselves counting the days until their kids leave home. And that makes them feel ashamed and embarrassed. Many have said, "I was a really nice person before I had kids. I never yelled at anyone." If you're in this situation, it's important to understand that what you're going through is a process that occurs naturally as our kids grow up to be adults. My intention with this book is to remove blame from the equation altogether. Whether you blame yourself or your teen, you're putting unnecessary obstacles in the way of change. No matter how disconnected from your teen you may feel you've become, the beauty of this technique is that it's never too late to repair that bond.

Empathy creates a bridge over troubled waters. Showing your child that you understand what he's experiencing is, in fact, the only way to strengthen the connection between you. And it isn't just about being nice; it's about changing the chemistry of your child's brain, since the feeling of being loved and understood releases the reward chemicals I cited above—the chemicals that cause us to bond with the person who is the source of those feelings.

If you already have a strong relationship with your teen and he or she is doing well, this program will help you strengthen and protect that bond and prepare your teen for the years ahead. If your child is angry, oppositional, highly emotional, and difficult to connect with, this book will provide strategies for repairing frayed bonds and help your child develop resilience and better emotional regulation.

Childhood is brief, but the teen years are even more fleeting. We want to spend those few years enjoying our teens instead of fighting with them. In this book I'll give you the tools—the information about brain functioning and development—to do that. I'll help you understand what's going on in your teenager's head and in the world he inhabits. With these tools in your pocket you'll be better able to appreciate why the techniques I teach are so effective for protecting and/or repairing the bond with your child—even if you worry that it's irreparably frayed—and why those same techniques will also help your teen change or control inappropriate, unacceptable, or downright dangerous behaviors.

The Power of Empathy

I experienced the power of empathy firsthand while I was still a student. I was working toward my master's degree in social work and interning at a mental health center for children and adolescents with learning disabilities. As interns we conducted initial interviews with the child's family while a team of psychologists, social workers, psychiatrists, and others, including our fellow interns, listened and watched from behind a one-way mirror. A phone had been placed in the interview room so that if the person doing the interview missed something, the people behind the mirror could pick up the phone to alert him. Needless to say, this was nerve-racking for the interviewer. I was terrified and, at the beginning, not a very good interviewer.

Another intern at the center had been there longer, had more experience, and was, at the time, a much better interviewer than I. Out of my own insecurity, I'd convinced myself that our supervisor liked her better than me. I felt threatened and inadequate (a lot like how a teenager feels much of the time, no matter how hard he or she tries to hide it), and my way of coping with those feelings was to act out by arriving thirty to forty-five minutes late for work on a fairly regular basis.

One morning, after I'd been late several days in a row and knew I was on thin ice, the elevator door opened and there was my supervisor. She asked me to come to her office for a minute, and I was worried. As I walked toward her office the hall seemed to get longer and longer. I was sure I knew what she was going to say: *This is not appropriate. This is a professional program. You're a master's candidate. This behavior is unacceptable.* At the same time I was thinking about everything I would say in response. Even though I knew she had every right to reprimand me, I felt the need to defend my behavior. But she didn't do that at all. Instead, she sat me down and said, "I've noticed you've been late a number of times, and I can't help wondering if there's something we're not doing here as an agency to support you. Somehow we're blowing it. There's something you need that we're not giving you. I think that's what you're trying to tell me by being late."

I was dumbfounded, so dumbfounded that I almost fell off my chair. And then I burst into tears.

I don't know about you, but I can't think of a time in my life when I was being yelled at or reprimanded and said, "Oh, thank you so much for straightening me out. I don't know what I was thinking. Let me work on changing that." When I'm being shouted at or criticized I become angry and resentful. Had my supervisor yelled at me as I expected, she would have confirmed all the negative thoughts about the program that I'd built up in my mind. I would have perceived her as mean and blamed everyone but myself for my own actions. But because she chose empathy, everything changed for me. Her words showed that she really wanted to understand my experience, and I was totally disarmed. I had no reason to be defensive, which meant that I was able to turn my energy inward and use it to gain insight into myself.

What my supervisor did in that conversation was to reflect my experience back to me—a technique called "mirroring" that lies at the heart of my Connected Parenting program—and by doing so she showed that she understood me. I've never forgotten that mirroring moment. It had a profoundly positive effect not only on my professional life but on me as a mother and a person. I knew in that instant that *this* was the way to change behavior.

What I didn't know then is that my supervisor's words were also having a powerful effect on my brain chemistry. She was connecting directly with the part of my brain that's responsible for mood control and bonding, which triggered the release of chemicals that calmed me and helped block the stress hormones that induce the fight-or-flight response.

Teenagers often respond no differently from the way I did that day. If they perceive you to be mean their energy will go into defending themselves, and you'll be either caught up in a vortex of escalating emotions or ignored entirely as they turn their backs on you and slam the door behind them. Discussing the problem, voicing your concerns, and offering guidance also have a very important place in creating behavioral change—and in the Connected Parenting model—but only when they come after empathy.

One of the most poignant lessons I ever learned about the power of listening and caring came in the context of a pilot project I was

involved in early in my career. The agency I was with had partnered
with the Hospital for Sick Children to work with young offenders
from lower income areas in the Toronto school system.

We knew that up to 75 percent of young offenders had learning
disabilities (LDs). (This, incidentally, is not the same as saying that
75 percent of children with learning disabilities will become young
offenders.) It's not hard to figure out what happens: the kids with
learning disabilities often do poorly in school and are therefore
more likely to drop out. They're frustrated, which increases their
anxiety, and they're angry. And they're the kids who are least likely
to have the perceptual and social skills that keep other kids from
getting caught.

We also knew that when a learning disability is diagnosed early
and the issue addressed, these children are no more likely than
others to become young offenders. But the ones who are diagnosed
early tend to come from stable, middle-class or affluent families, so,
once again, the odds are skewed against kids from poorer communi-
ties. In addition, kids from the wrong side of the tracks tend to move
more often, so if their school has targeted them for testing and
they're on a list, by the time their name comes up they're likely to
have moved on. As a result, their disability is never identified. Often
by the time they get to high school they've already been in trouble.
At that point the school authorities generally react to the behavior
rather than to the circumstances or the LD that underlies it.

It was (and is) a vicious cycle, and it was my agency's hope that
our pilot project would bring more awareness to the problem. The
study focused on young male offenders who were on probation and
had a history of academic and behavioral trouble. These were
tough kids who'd seen and done a lot of awful things. They'd been
neglected, often abused. They'd probably been labeled as individuals to fear and stay away from. The school selected the likely
candidates among its students, and a psychologist tested them for

learning disabilities—which, not surprisingly, almost all of them turned out to have. Those with LDs were then invited into the study. Half the kids got the service immediately and the other half—the control group—had to wait a year before they got it. I was the on-site counselor, and my service included working with the boys individually, acting as a liaison and advocate for them with their teachers and probation officers, and training the teachers and probation officers to understand LDs and the social and emotional issues associated with them. The boys also participated in weekly group therapy sessions offered by other therapists on the team.

The first thing we did was to sit down with each student, explain what his learning disability actually was, and help him understand how it affected him academically, behaviorally, and emotionally. Most of these boys had spent their entire life believing they were stupid (even though, on some level, they knew they were smart) because they were never able to demonstrate their intelligence in school. In fact, a person has to test average or above average in intelligence in order to be diagnosed with a learning disability in the first place. Most of the kids I worked with were so excited to learn that they were in the 80th percentile in verbal reasoning or the 90th percentile for nonverbal spatial awareness that they weren't even concerned about the areas in which they tested lower. They were astounded to hear that they weren't "stupid" after all. Some of them actually cried.

We did a huge amount of mirroring to let them know that we understood where they were coming from and what they were going through. These kids were angry. They had seen social workers and therapists all their lives and thought of us all as the enemy. For most of them the term "social services" almost always meant that some stranger was interfering in their home life, taking babies from their mothers, and generally exerting unwanted authority over them.

Instead of starting out as most people would—"You must be very angry. My job is to help you tell me what's wrong."—I began our conversations by saying, "You don't want to be here. I'm a social worker and you don't want to have anything to do with me." I went on to state out loud what their facial expressions and body language were telling me they were feeling. Their reactions were amazing. First they'd say something like "Yo, Miss, I don't know why you care so much; no one has ever cared about me like this." And before I knew it they were spilling their whole life story.

All the boys who received the service completed the school year. Most of them did well enough to be promoted, and a few received the first As of their entire life. Of those in the control group, 70 percent dropped out, so we knew the program was successful for those in the service. Unfortunately we couldn't get the funding to continue; for whatever reason, no one seems to want to spend money helping young offenders.

But the point of all this is to tell you about Adam, one of the most amazing kids I've ever met. Adam volunteered for the study. He'd beaten another teen severely and then turned himself in to the police, saying "I'm going to kill somebody and I need some help before I do." He had served time in juvenile detention and was now back in school. He had also been the head of a gang and had quit. (If you know anything about gangs, you know this is almost impossible to do.) When he met me he said, "You know, Miss, you know what it's like to go from having three thousand dollars in your pocket all the time to wearing shitty clothes and looking like hell?" But he'd done it. He'd given everything up to come back to school and change his life. He was truly a remarkable kid, but he could also blow up at any second and was on the verge of being expelled. He'd tested very high in nonverbal skills but just average in verbal, so not only were his grades suffering but also he wasn't as good as some other kids at talking himself out of a tight spot.

One day a substitute teacher took over his class. Adam had been talking, so the teacher went up to him and began shaking a finger in his face. Adam stood up and smacked the teacher's hand away, the teacher hit the emergency button, and Adam was escorted to the principal's office. The principal was a remarkable man. The students admired him and he cared deeply about them, but he had picked out Adam as a troublemaker. He was concerned because so many teachers had complained that Adam intimidated them.

I happened to be in the building that day and someone came to find me. I started to mirror with Adam, using compassion and understanding before lecturing or correcting, and by doing that I helped him calm down enough to explain why he'd done what he did. This is the story he told me and the principal.

He'd been taught practically since birth that if someone gets in your face you need to get them out of your face, because if you don't you lose status in the community. Those were the rules of the street plain and simple, and the rules of the street took precedence over the rules of the school, since your safety and status depended on understanding and obeying them. One day, he said, when he was nine or ten years old, a bigger kid—maybe thirteen—spat on his sister and his father told him to go out there and beat the kid up. Adam didn't want to do it. He was scared, but he went because it was his duty. The whole neighborhood turned out to watch, cheer, and egg the two boys on. The fight lasted about forty-five minutes until someone finally stopped it. Adam was much smaller but he fought hard. By the end his eyes were streaming with tears, but he never gave up. He was exhausted by the ordeal and told us that all he really wanted was for his dad to pick him up, comfort him, and carry him home. But instead his father slapped him hard on the back, said "Good work," reminded him not to be a sucker, and walked away. "So that's what my life is like," Adam said. "That's what I've been taught to do; that's what I have to do."

As Adam finished his story I looked up, and there was the principal standing silently with tears in his eyes—the same principal who'd been about to kick Adam out of school. For the first time he understood not just this particular kid but all the other kids whom he'd previously perceived only as troublemakers. He understood that they were caught between two conflicting cultures: one where you were expected to do right by your friends and your neighborhood and the other where you were expected to do right by the school.

Based on that one moment of clarity, everything began to change for both Adam and the principal. Adam saw not pity but pure understanding and compassion in the principal's eyes, and he felt understood possibly for the first time in his life. He took responsibility for his behavior with the substitute teacher, and said that he knew he needed help but would work hard to reconcile his two worlds. He gave us permission to share not only that story but other details of his life with his teachers. They began to look at him differently, and he began to look at them differently. They tried harder to reach him and build a relationship with him. They got to know the remarkable young man who lived behind the tough facade.

In the end, Adam was able to say, "Okay, I don't really understand these school rules, but I know I have to follow them if I want to fit in here. So I'm going to have my rules for out there and my rules for in here." He got it, but not because of lecturing and punishing. He got it because he felt understood.

I'm happy to say that Adam finished school, moved out of the inner city, and is now a carpenter in a small town outside Toronto. He wrote me a letter not long ago telling me that I had changed his life and that if it weren't for me and the people in the program he'd probably be dead. He's probably right, and he isn't the only kid in that program for whom that's true. But he changed my life, too.

He taught me that the technique I'm going to teach you, although difficult at times, allows you to see the best in people and bring about change from the inside out. If it can work with kids like Adam, it can certainly work with moody teenagers who don't necessarily come from troubled backgrounds but who are confused, overwhelmed, and aloof.

Practicing connected-parenting techniques allows me to see the best in people every day. That's a gift to me, and it can also be a gift to you and your teen.

ONE

What's Going On in
Your Teenager's Brain

Until relatively recently, it was generally accepted that brain development was largely governed by genetics—that is, nature—and that whatever effect nurture had on the brain was mostly limited to the first five years of life. We believed that much of the brain's construction took place in those early years, during which personality traits and intelligence were pretty much set in stone. After that, or so we thought, the brain was hardwired and there wasn't a lot we could do to change it.

More recently, however, technologies like MRIs and CAT scans have enabled us to learn much more about neuroplasticity—the brain's ability to change and adapt to its environment by creating and maintaining the wiring that supports optimal reactions to the external world. In other words, the brain changes in response to experience, not only in its physical structure but also in its functional organization. We're discovering that the brain continues to make new connections and rewire itself throughout our entire life. And while the first major neurological growth spurt occurs during infancy and early childhood, researchers have found that a second significant period of brain development occurs beginning in adolescence and continuing into young adulthood.

The Importance of Mirroring and Attachment

When a baby is born, her initial experiences are essentially limited to interactions with her parents, and particularly her mother. The way a baby begins to learn about the world is related to what's called the mirror neuron system. Until the mid-1990s, when a group of neuroscientists in Italy discovered the way mirror neurons function, it was believed that humans basically learned by doing. Since then we've come to understand that the same learning experience occurs simply by watching—and mirroring—the behaviors we observe. So when you smile, coo, and make funny faces at your baby, she learns to copy you. She also learns that a particular action on her part initiates a reliable response from you. And all the while the baby's brain is creating more and more neuropathways, or connections, that ultimately determine how she responds to what's going on in her world.

Scientists now believe that the mirror neuron system is responsible for the acquisition of not only language and motor skills but also social skills, including our ability to empathize with others. In the words of Dr. Giacomo Rizzolatti, who led the team that made the initial discovery, "Mirror neurons allow us to grasp the minds of others not through conceptual reasoning but through direct stimulation. By feeling, not by thinking."

By mirroring and reflecting his feelings back to him, we parents are letting our child know that we love and understand him; we are creating an attachment bond between us. We're also helping him organize his own feelings by seeing them mirrored in our expressions and body language. As Daniel Siegel notes in his book *The Developing Mind*, "For the infant and young child, attachment relationships are a major environmental factor that shapes development of the brain's maximum growth. Attachment establishes interpersonal relationships that help the immature brain use the mature functions of the parent's brain to organize its own processes." So, mirroring has a twofold function: it creates that all-important bond that lets our baby know he's safe with us, and it allows him to develop appropriate responses to his immediate environment.

In his book *Scattered Minds*, physician and drug-addiction authority Gabor Maté writes, "For the infant there exists no abstract, 'out-there' reality. The emotional milieu with which we surround the child is the world as he experiences it." And in the words of child psychiatrist and researcher Margaret Mahler, "For the newborn the parent is the principal representative of the world. To the infant and toddler the world reveals itself in the image of the parent—eye contact, intensity, body language, tone of voice ... Whatever the parent's intention, these are means by which the child receives most of her formative communication skills."

In a 2004 *New Yorker* essay by Malcolm Gladwell entitled "The Ketchup Conundrum," psychophysicist and market researcher Howard Moskowitz quotes an old Yiddish saying: "To a worm in horseradish the world is horseradish." With no disrespect intended, in the context of child development, your infant is the worm and you are the horseradish.

When you're stressed, your baby senses and absorbs that stress; when you respond to him with joy, he senses your mood and responds joyfully. Gabor Maté illustrates the intense relationship between adult and child with the following story. He was born in 1944 in Hungary, just at the time it was being occupied by the Nazis. His mother was so concerned that her infant wouldn't stop crying that she called the pediatrician, who told her, "All my Jewish babies are crying."

I don't mean to make anyone feel guilty about being stressed or responding in less than optimal ways to their baby at one time or another. The point is to help you understand how tuned in your baby is to your emotional channel, how dependent he is on you for his brain development, and how important it is to make and maintain those connections that promote optimal brain growth, not only at birth but throughout a child's life.

We're all stressed from time to time; we all get short-tempered. The good news is that, because the brain is so malleable, or plastic, and so capable of adapting to experience, we can also make amends, repair, and redo what we may not have done as well as we would have liked the first time. The beauty of the parenting model I teach is that it's so forgiving.

The Limbic System, Cortisol, and Oxytocin

The limbic system is the part of the brain that, among its many functions, deals with intense emotions such as fear and pleasure. It sets the emotional tone of the mind, attaches emotional importance to external events, and stores highly charged memories. Oxytocin and cortisol are brain chemicals that are triggered or released in the hypothalamus, which is part of the limbic system. In recent years researchers have shown how particular experiences or environmental stimuli affect the release of these and other brain chemicals.

Sometimes called the love hormone, the attachment hormone, or the tend-and-befriend hormone, oxytocin has been linked to social bonding as well as to feelings of serenity and security. Its release is triggered in women giving birth and is associated with the instinctive love a mother feels for her baby. But oxytocin is also released in the brain when we feel we are loved. In other words, when a baby feels her mother's love, oxytocin is released in her brain. It works both ways, and is therefore believed to be responsible for creating the initial bond that mother and child feel for each other. That bond is nature's way of ensuring the survival of the species. No other animal is as helpless at birth; no other animal's brain takes so long to develop fully—and for the frontal lobes, this development can take up to twenty-five years. Since pushing a twenty-five-year-old through the birth canal would be highly unpleasant, nature has made certain that the human infant bonds with a parent (or parents) who can protect him until he's fully capable of protecting himself.

The power of oxytocin has yet to be fully revealed, but several studies have shown its powerful effects. One study, conducted by Paul J. Zak and colleagues at the Center for Neuroeconomics Studies at Claremont Graduate University, indicated that when participants were given a sum of money and encouraged to invest it with a stranger, they initially invested only a quarter to a third of the total amount. But after four sniffs of intranasal oxytocin their trust level skyrocketed to the point where they unhesitatingly became willing to invest 80 percent or more. Another study, published in the journal *Progress in Neurobiology*, showed that couples receiving intranasal oxytocin prior to a conflict discussion displayed significantly increased positive communication behaviors. And a small study conducted by French scientists at the Center for Scientific Research and published online in the *Proceedings of the National Academy of Science* found that when adults with either a high-functioning form of autism or Asperger's syndrome inhaled oxytocin in a nasal spray they scored significantly higher on a test that involved recognizing faces and in a game that involved tossing a ball with other people. According to Angela Sirigu, who led the study, "It's possible it can become a cure, if it's given early when the problems are detected in little kids. We can change the way these patients interact with people from childhood."

Cortisol, on the other hand, is activated during periods of stress. The hypothalamus manufactures a corticotropin-releasing hormone (CRH), which stimulates the pituitary gland to release adreno-corticotropic hormone (ACTH), and this, in turn, causes the adrenal glands to secrete cortisol in the blood. Cortisol is present at high levels during periods of fight-or-flight, the physiological response that occurs instinctively when we sense that we're in immediate danger. Our body is put on a state of high alert. Our breathing and heart rate quicken, our muscles tighten, and we become hyper-vigilant. Our body is entirely focused on repelling the threat, and other, non-essential functions are slowed down.

The fight-or-flight reaction is useful in those times when we're truly in danger and need to direct all our mental and physical energy toward escaping a marauding tiger or an onrushing train. But incessant stress leads to a constantly elevated level of cortisol in the bloodstream, which has been linked to both cognitive impairment and the inhibition of oxytocin release.

Both bonding and mood, then, are regulated by the same part of the brain—the limbic system. The implication of this relationship is fascinating. It means that the more you feel bonded to another person, the more capable you are of regulating your own mood. And the more you're able to control your mood, the more other people will want to bond with you. Conversely, the more detached you are the more stressed you become, and the less able you are to think clearly and to feel the sense of calm and security that comes with being bonded to another human being.

These facts of brain chemistry are pivotal to how and why connected parenting is so effective.

The Darwinian Brain

When a baby is upset, or hungry, or wet, he sends out a signal—usually by screaming or crying—to let you know something is wrong. You respond by holding him, by making soothing noises, or simply through your facial expressions and body language to let him know that his message has been received and understood. By doing that you're mirroring his feelings back to him, saying (without actually putting it into words), *I understand what you're feeling, but I'm okay, I'm not upset, and I can help you with that.* This mirroring bypasses the language center of the brain. The baby recognizes his own emotional state in the facial expression and voice of his caregiver. When he does that, his brain releases reward chemicals that cause him to calm down and stop crying because he knows someone else is going to deal with the problem. He knows that his message has been accurately received, noted, and acknowledged. Without being conscious of it, you're changing his behavior by mirroring. Most of us do this instinctively with babies. We lean in, copy his facial expression, and demonstrate that his message is being registered. We don't look at the baby and say, "Oh for heaven's sake, it's just a wet diaper! Why are you getting so upset? We do this twenty times a day!"

It's not until the toddler years that we're more likely to try to change or control a child's behavior without first signaling that we understand the problem. In terms of brain development, however, both are equally important: just as we did for our infant, we need to create an environment for our older children that reflects a balance between mirroring and containing.

Why is this the case? Because the brain is constantly changing in order to function most efficiently and therefore survive. Basically, what's going on is a kind of neuro-Darwinism: the person whose brain is best adapted to its environment is the one who will thrive.

So if a child is born in a war zone, for example, his brain will adjust to deal with the stress and to survive in a hostile environment. It will be in a constant state of fight-or-flight rather than dealing with mood regulation. Ideally, we want to create a home environment that's exactly the opposite. We want to give our child those positive experiences that bathe his brain in oxytocin and allow him to calm down, feel love, and develop trust. Mirroring is the way to do that.

The Toddler in a Teenage Body

The two periods in a child's development when behavioral problems are most likely to manifest are the toddler years and the adolescent years. I believe this happens for two reasons: it is during these periods that the brain undergoes a neurological growth spurt and that attachment issues are most likely to occur.

As your baby becomes a toddler—and literally starts to toddle around—he's creating those neuropathways that allow him to learn how to walk. Although it seems as if Jamie just gets up and takes his first steps one day, his brain has been busy learning to walk for some time. You may have had the same kind of experience doing the Sunday crossword puzzle or trying to master a new piece on the piano. You get stuck and walk away, and then, when you come back later, you find that you can fill in the blank or play the chord you'd been stuck on. Your brain was working on solving the problem even when you thought you weren't thinking about it. In the same way, the toddler's brain is constantly busy creating the connections that allow him to master new skills. The effort can be stressful, and that's one of the reasons he may be extra-cranky or whiny at times—the stage we've come to think of as the Terrible Twos.

And while he's learning all that, he's also beginning to separate from you. He's exploring new things and new places, even if he's only emptying the pots out of the kitchen cupboard or going into the next room. He *needs* to move away from you and expand his horizons, but he also needs to know he's still attached to you. So the behaviors that may be driving you nuts result from both the neurological growth spurt and the stress that gets put on his attachment to you while he's in the process of separating and becoming an individual.

To complicate matters, this is also the time when we begin to drop our natural mirroring and begin to tell the child what we think he *should* be feeling or thinking. For example, if our little one comes to us and says "I'm hungry," we're increasingly likely to say something like, "That's impossible. You can't be hungry. You just ate," which leaves the child thinking, *Well, that's weird. I thought I was hungry.*

If you're wondering what all this has to do with your adolescent, let me ask you this: Have you ever thought or said to your teen, "My god, you're acting just like a two-year-old"? Well, you're right! At times a teen's behaviors aren't very different from those of a toddler. There are times when you can't reason with a teen any better than you can with a two-year-old, only now he's much bigger and his tantrums can seem a lot scarier. I often tell my clients that when their teenager is screaming at them or slamming out of a room, they should try to imagine him with a two-year-old's head on his teenage body. What he's experiencing neurologically and developmentally is similar to what a toddler experiences—only more so. And just like that toddler, if he sends out an emotional message and doesn't see it registering on your face, he'll get more and more upset and send the message more and more forcefully in order to convince you how upsetting the situation really is. Except that now it's not more juice that he wants, it's permission to go to an unsupervised party at his friend's house.

While the toddler's monumental neurological growth spurt can make him cranky or whiny, the adolescent's can make him oppositional, sullen, or silent. Because there's so much going on in his brain, he can become overwhelmed and fly into a rage that makes it impossible to reason with him. His brain goes into fight-or-flight mode, adrenaline is pumping, and nothing you say is getting through, because the only thing on his mind is the need to protect himself from the perceived threat—which, in that moment, could very well be you. When a toddler throws a tantrum it may be upsetting or exasperating, but a teenage temper tantrum can be a lot more frightening and a lot less tolerable.

Teens can create an enormous amount of emotional noise, but that's all it is, noise—like the static on your radio when it isn't tuned properly or the growling noises a puppy uses to make himself seem bigger and badder than he really is. So, for example, if you ask your teenage son to please hang up his coat, the response you might get is "ARRGHBLAHHHWHAAH!" If you get sucked into reacting to the noise and scream back, he'll make even more noise. He'll have his fit and then he'll feel better because he's gotten rid of all that pent-up emotion. But you won't feel better. You'll be standing there in the aftermath of the battle feeling frustrated and wondering what happened.

I generally tell my clients that when their toddler is spiraling into a vortex of emotions they should just disengage, while assuring him that he'll be okay and that they'll be back to check on him soon. The same advice works for a teen. If he hasn't already stormed out of the room, the best thing you can do is refuse to engage in what will only become an escalating battle.

We often talk about how oppositional teens are when in fact it's their *job* to be oppositional. Just as when he was a toddler, he's in the process of separating from you and asserting his individuality. Only now, instead of going into another room to play with his toys, he's going out into the big wide world, which is even scarier. You may think he wants to leave you behind, but he doesn't. He still wants and needs to know that he's attached to you, and that you're the place of safety to which he can always return.

Teens are engaged in a constant struggle between pushing and pulling. They're pushing you away one minute and then pulling you in. It's as if they are saying "I hate you/I love you, I need you/I don't need you" all at once. If those mixed messages are confusing for you, think how confusing the emotions that create them are for your teen. So when she's screaming "No I won't go and you can't make me!," just remind yourself that this is the kind of noise a frightened puppy makes. It's bluff, it's bravado, and you need to resist the urge to scream back, "Yes you are and yes I can!" If you're able to remain calm, stay neutral, and simply say, "I hear you. And I'm going to leave you alone for a minute because I don't think you're in a place where I can help you, but I know you're a good kid and I'm sure you'll make the right choice. I'll see you in the car in a few minutes," she'll probably appear in the car. The more you push, the more you're giving your teen something to push back against, because as we all learned in physics class, every action has an equal and opposite reaction. But if you refuse to push, she'll have nothing to push back against. In the words of Gabor Maté, "A person can be oppositional only when there's something to be oppositional against."

The concept of attachment can be compared to rock climbing with a partner. The person on the ground is wearing a harness with a rope. The other end of the rope is looped through a metal ring on the wall and then attached to the climber's harness. The rope connects the climber to his partner on the ground, who gives him just enough slack to move upward. Because the climber trusts his partner and feels the tension on the rope and the safety it provides, he'll have the confidence to reach farther and climb higher, knowing he can't fall. But the tension needs to be just right: too much and the climber can't move, too little and he can't feel the connection. The real trick, then, is to give your teen the rope he needs to separate from you while still letting him know that he is and always will be connected to you in a positive, loving way.

Neurologist Ron Clavier uses a different analogy in his book *Teen Brain, Teen Mind*. He compares parenting an adolescent to being in the NASA mission control center in Houston. Your teens are like astronauts orbiting in space, and you're the home base to which they return for guidance and security. You need to be brave enough to let them be out there, understanding that, although they're separating from you physically, they're still attached to you emotionally.

Separating Isn't Easy

Parents often complain that their teens are insulting to them, that they don't want to be seen with them, or that they're embarrassed by them. I know this kind of rejection can be hurtful, but hard as it may be to bear, it's simply part of the normal separation process. You shouldn't take it personally.

It's much easier to pull away from something you don't like than it is to separate from something to which you're attached. If you've ever left a job, for example, you may have noticed that the minute you made your decision to leave, you started to think about everything you disliked about the job. You were already beginning the separation process, and that's what your teen is doing when he criticizes or insults you. I know it's rude, but if you get offended and allow yourself to respond by saying things like "What do you mean? I'm your mother. You can't talk to me like that, after all I've done for you!" you're actually feeding into the behavior by fighting on his level, and he'll push back even harder. If you can accept it as a normal (if unpleasant) and temporary developmental stage, I assure you it will pass.

If you do feel the need to respond to your teen's criticism of your clothing choices, your taste in music, your hairstyle, or pretty much anything else, in a neutral and matter-of-fact voice, try to say something like "I get it. I felt exactly the same way when I was your age, but I'm just fine with the way my hair looks and the music I listen to." By letting him know he can't hurt you, you're making a stand-up-for-yourself statement, exactly as I suggest teens do when they're being bullied by a peer (see Chapter Seven). It will work just as well when you're being bullied by your child.

That said, there are of course some behaviors that your teen does need help correcting. Once you understand why those behaviors occur and how to employ the techniques I use with my clients, you'll be able to correct them from a place of love, without being perceived as mean and without creating even more tension.

Thinking and Perspective: The Role of the Frontal Lobes

It's important to keep in mind that the frontal lobes, which are responsible for thinking, planning, reasoning, and interpreting social signals, haven't yet matured in the teenage brain. As I mentioned earlier, recent studies have shown that the frontal lobes aren't developed until somewhere around the age of twenty-five. When neuroscientists led by Elizabeth Sowell of the University of California Los Angeles' Lab of Neuro Imaging used MRIs to compare the brains of twelve- to sixteen-year-olds with those of twenty-somethings, they found that the frontal lobes undergo their greatest change between puberty and young adulthood.

One function of the frontal lobes is to interpret, mediate, and process primal emotions so that we react in an appropriate manner. When they're not fully formed, they may not be mediating feelings appropriately. Joe Dispenza articulates the problem in his book *Evolve Your Brain*. Teens, he says, "do not yet have the hardware to process complex reasoning. Their frontal lobes are still developing, and at the same time their amygdala, which sits deep in the midbrain and is involved in their gut reactions and their fight-or-flight responses, is more active than the higher centers for reason, such as the frontal lobes ... The frontal lobes cannot hold the reins of the emotional self." In other words, teens don't think so much as feel. The frontal lobes function as the CEOs or policemen of the brain. Their job is to constantly suppress those feelings and control impulses—not so easy for a brain that has yet to fully develop this ability.

Even adults when they're upset can say something they later regret, so think how much harder it must be for teens to step back and view the situation from the other person's perspective. It's something we expect of our teens because they look smart enough, tall enough, and old enough to do it. But often they can't, and they need us to model appropriate behavior and provide the guidance and compassion necessary to help them develop that very important ability.

Why does all this matter? For two reasons: First, it explains why teens are always going into fight-or-flight mode and flying off the handle for no good reason—or at least no good reason that we can appreciate. They're reacting emotionally without thinking about whether their reaction is appropriate to the situation. Second, it explains why mirroring and connecting on the *emotional* level is the *only* way we can communicate effectively with them.

Counteracting Automatic Negative Thoughts

In his book *Change Your Brain, Change Your Life*, Daniel Amen, a clinical neuroscientist and child and adolescent psychiatrist, discusses the role of automatic negative thoughts, or ANTS. What he means by this is that when we have a thought, our brain sends out a chemical message that matches that thought. If the thought is negative—*I look terrible* or *I'm going to fail the test* or *I don't have any friends*—our brain will be sending out stress hormones like cortisol that reinforce those beliefs and organize the brain around that negativity. So, what we need to do—both for ourselves and for our children—is learn to recognize ANTS for what they are: annoying creations of our own mind. Once we've done that we can counteract ANTS with positive thoughts, such as *I look great. People are going to look at me and think I look great* or *I studied for that test. I know the material* or *I have some really good friends who love me*.

Sometimes ANTS are created by what Amen calls mind-reading. For example, if someone seems to be less friendly toward us than usual, we'll automatically assume he or she is angry with us rather than thinking, *Gee, she's in a bad mood. I wonder what's up with her?* In other words, we assume we're somehow to blame for the other person's mood. Instead we need to come up with an alternative reason for the behavior. *Maybe she had a fight with her boyfriend, or maybe she's just having a bad hair day.* In this way we wash the brain with positive chemicals such as oxytocin. And when we make a habit of it, we're actually changing our brain chemistry and creating new neuropathways, which means we'll be less likely to fall victim to ANTS in the future.

There are two more things to understand about ANTS. First, when we have automatic negative thoughts about another person, our brain sends out the same negative chemicals as when we have those thoughts about ourselves, which is why thinking bad thoughts can make us feel a bit queasy or sick to our stomach. Second, we don't actually have to believe our positive thoughts when we use them to counteract our ANTS. They'll have the same chemical effect on the brain whether we believe them or not. And once they change our brain chemistry, we actually become much more likely to believe them.

But as we've seen, if something arouses a teen's anger or makes him anxious, the part of the brain that ought to kick in and say, *Now wait a minute, this isn't really so bad. What am I so upset about?* isn't yet up to speed. And since he lacks the ability to get a better sense of perspective, the negative thought can run amok: *Oh my god! This is horrible; no one's ever going to be my friend again. I'll have to leave town. This is the absolute worst thing that's ever happened to me in my entire life!*

In his discussion of attention deficit disorder, Gabor Maté notes that some people have extremely intense reactions to relatively mild stimuli, in much the same way that people who are allergic have extreme reactions to physical stimuli. He calls this type of hypersensitivity an "emotional allergy." Because teens are often so touchy (for all the reasons we've already discussed) and because their frontal lobes aren't yet developed enough to moderate these reactions, it may be useful to think of them as emotionally allergic. There's no point in trying to reason them out of their (to you ridiculous) maelstrom of emotions, since if the reasoning part of their brain were working the way it should they wouldn't have gotten into that state in the first place. So you need to bypass the frontal lobes and address the limbic system directly, which is exactly what happens when you mirror. Remember what Dr. Rizzolatti said about the mirror neuron system: It allows us "to grasp the minds of others not through conceptual reasoning but through direct stimulation. By feeling, not by thinking."

By appealing directly to the emotional center of your teenager's brain, you're sending the message that you empathize with what he's feeling. This allows him to calm down because he can feel the tension on the rope that lets him know you're there to keep him from falling. And *then*, but only then, you can begin to explain *why* whatever he wants or feels or hates or is so furious about isn't appropriate. In other words, you take over the role of his frontal lobes until his are developed. You use your own reasoning abilities to help him become better at regulating his emotions.

This doesn't mean he's suddenly going to be completely reasonable and understanding: he'll still be mad and he'll probably still tell you that his life has been ruined. But he'll get over it, probably faster than you would have expected.

So now you have some idea of what's going on inside your teenager's brain, and what you can do to let him know you're there to help him gain control of his emotions so that he can think more clearly and make better choices. Since those choices are being made in the context of the larger world, we now need to take a closer look at that world—which probably isn't quite the same as the world in which you grew up.

TWO

The World They Live In

What's going on inside her brain comprises the teenager's interior environment, but her brain is ultimately influenced by what's happening in the world around her.

The world teens live in today is both more permissive and more sheltered than the world we grew up in. They're exposed to all kinds of information and subjected to all kinds of pressures we didn't have to cope with. While this means they may be wiser and more sophisticated than we were, it also means they're expected to process information and make difficult decisions that create an enormous amount of stress.

Too Much, Too Soon

The world is scary. Just watching the evening news is enough to raise the blood pressure and increase the stress level of any adult, so what do you think it's doing to your kid? Bad things are happening to good kids all the time, and your kids know it. They may act as if none of it bothers them, but all that scary stuff is triggering the release of stress hormones that affect the brain.

The world may not be any more dangerous than it was, say, twenty years ago—some statistics suggest that it may even be safer—but because we have so much more access to information, and fearful images are coming at us by way of our televisions and computers virtually nonstop, it *appears* to be more frightening. This disconnect between perception and reality is something we can easily discuss with our teens. And we can use what we see in the media as a way to introduce the concept that our perceptions of what other people think of us may not always be accurate either.

In addition to the stress created by the news media, there's the pressure from advertisers and merchandisers to conform and consume. Because most kids are so incredibly egocentric, they're certain that everyone is looking at them and judging them. Being accepted is monumentally important to teenagers. They're in constant fear of getting it wrong and looking dumb. We've all worried from time to time about what we should wear or how we should behave on a particular occasion. Well, that's how adolescents feel almost all the time, which makes them perfect targets for anyone who wants to sell them something. And parents, perhaps because they remember that feeling or because they're afraid to say no, often give in, even when they know it's the wrong thing to do. (It's a lot easier to deal with a toddler's meltdown in the toy store because you refuse to buy her a Barbie lunch box than it is to cope with a teenager's rage in the department store because you won't buy her a pair of designer jeans.)

Admittedly, it's harder to say no in a world where permissiveness is the norm. When your kid says he *has* to have something because *everyone else* has it, he's probably telling the truth. But if you're constantly there to smooth away every obstacle in his path, give in to his every whim, and basically allow him to believe he's the center of the universe, you really aren't doing him any favors.

The Perils of Overprotection

Ironically, while our kids live in a more permissive society, they have a lot *less* freedom than we did. They're constantly connected to their parents via the umbilical cord of the cellphone. And while it may be comforting for parents to know they can contact their child when they need to (and vice versa)—there are certainly positive aspects to the use of all this technology—this connectedness creates a strange new dependence on the kids' part and gives parents a false sense of security.

Kids may text their parents twenty or more times a day with every little problem or thought that pops into their head, which means parents are solving micro-problems all day long. All that calling and texting leads parents to believe that they know where their children are and what they're doing. But they don't, of course. If you're calling or texting your kid every five minutes, he's eventually going to resent it and stop picking up the phone—and believe me, kids can come up with all sorts of reasons why they couldn't answer. (You've probably done the same thing yourself.) And they can certainly lie about where they are.

You've probably heard of "helicopter" parents—moms—who hover over their children night and day. Danish child psychologist Bent Hougaard coined his own evocative term for this phenomenon. He calls them "curling parents." If you've ever watched the Winter Olympics, you may have seen athletes competing in the centuries-old sport of curling. It involves two teams of four people each who take turns sliding smooth, heavy stones down a sheet of ice toward a target painted on the ice surface. As the stone approaches the target, one or two teammates use brooms to franti-cally sweep the ice in front of the stone to make it move faster and change direction. The sport provides a wonderful visual image of the way many parents attempt to improve their child's chances of becoming a "winner." The curling approach teaches the child that he can't reach the target on his own and that he needs his parents to clear the ice in front of him in order to succeed.

And these days, that habit of overprotection is continuing after kids go off to university. In an interview published in the Toronto *Globe and Mail*, Joseph Allen, co-author of *Escaping the Endless Adolescence: How We Can Help Our Teenagers Grow Up Before They Grow Old*, provides a disturbing statistic. "The average [U.S.] college senior is in touch with their parents more than 13 times a week. And it's not because they have such close relationships. It's because they're getting help—from picking courses to editing papers to parents reminding them of deadlines." A friend of mine even called the counselor at her son's university to ask who was going to wake him up in the morning so that he wouldn't miss his classes!

Parents may even go on hovering once their kids have entered the job market. Some companies, when training new hires, distribute a "parent packet" with information explaining what the young adult will be doing on the job, what benefits she'll receive, and details of the company's health insurance plan. These compa-nies created the packets because their human resources depart-ments were being inundated with phone calls from parents checking to see if their son or daughter was adjusting well to the new job.

If you think those situations are normal, sadly you're not wrong, but you may also need to rethink the way you've been preparing your child for adulthood. Neither hovering nor sweeping builds resilience and independence in a child of any age. Rather, this overprotective behavior creates an unhealthy reliance that leads kids to believe they're incapable of solving their own problems. That feeling ultimately makes them more fearful, less empowered— and more likely to be influenced, for better or worse, by their peers. This is not the kind of healthy connection I'm talking about.

Facing her own challenges, with a loving, consistent, nurturing caregiver there to lend support, can actually make the child's brain stronger, because it helps her compare and scale her experiences along a continuum. Years ago, when adolescents were more likely to be exposed to disappointment (because parents weren't so quick to intervene), they were more likely to develop a realistic under-standing of the obstacles they came up against. They learned what was bad and what was *really* bad. So when they encountered a problem of some kind they were able to step back, compare it to something else they'd dealt with, and say, "Well, this isn't really so bad compared to that [whatever that might have been]." But if they have no experience of the "really bad," they're more likely to become anxious and overwhelmed by the smallest impediment.

I sometimes compare overly protective parents to people who compulsively use hand sanitizer. If we don't allow ourselves to be exposed to a germ or two, we won't build up any resistance to infec-tion. In the same way, the easier life gets, the more likely it is that the brain will make a big deal out of the least little problem.

Even my daughter Zoë, who's usually sensible and not a kid I'd call a drama queen, had her moment when she came home from her dance class's Christmas party, flung herself across the sofa, and began sobbing because her secret Santa had given her a collection of bath products. She'd put a lot of thought into her own secret Santa gift and couldn't believe she'd received such a "lame" present. My first inclination was to say, "Are you kidding me? You're crying over a bath kit? Do you have any idea how ridiculous that is?" But of course I knew that in the midst of her hysteria I'd only be making things worse. So we had a little mirroring moment about how disappointed she was and how much thought she'd put into her secret Santa gift. As she started to calm down I was able to start a dialogue about all the truly terrible things people have to go through and help her to see the bigger picture. And sure enough, she came back later and said, "You know, I can't believe what an idiot I was. I can't believe I did that."

In addition to creating dependence and anxiety, however, all that hovering, nudging, and sweeping puts even more pressure on kids who already have about as much as they can deal with. This generation of teens has spent all their lives hearing that they've got to get good grades, they've got to get into a good college or university, they've got to get a good job. We parents—admittedly with the best of intentions—are continually letting our children know what they're going to be or should become, and in the process we too often forget what they are right now.

Hyper Parents & Coddled Kids, a documentary that aired in Canada in 2010, described the children born after 1980 as the all-time most privileged, cherished, and invested-in generation. Paradoxically, though, they're far from being the most secure generation ever. They feel both entitled and anxious. First-year college students are now coping with levels of anxiety comparable to those that got people hospitalized in the 1970s. Young people today say they feel as if they're carrying the weight of the world on their shoulders. If they receive a low grade they feel they're letting their parents down. If they get a poor performance review from their supervisor, or if something doesn't go as expected, they find themselves unable to cope.

I saw this connection between anxiety and entitlement play out in truly mind-boggling style with one of my young clients. She was the classic cherished only child whose parents did everything they could to ensure she'd be a star—and she was, except that she hadn't done any of it on her own. Once she got to college, where Mom and Dad weren't there to do her work for her, she started to fall apart. Because they hadn't wanted their little girl to live in a dorm where other kids might not be taking their work seriously enough and she might get distracted, they bought her an apartment and gave her an enormous monthly allowance. Two or three months into her freshman year my client began to be late for classes, and when her professors spoke to her about it she was offended and indignant. After a while she stopped turning in her written assignments. Before long she was failing her courses, and by the end of the year she had flunked out.

She couldn't bring herself to tell her parents. So she stayed in her apartment, collected her allowance, and started to experiment with drugs. When the next semester rolled around her parents sent her the tuition money and she simply cashed the check. This went on, unbelievably, for *three years* before the guilt finally got to her and she confessed what she'd done. Her mother called me for help. She told me it was as if their entire world had flipped upside down and every dream they'd had for their daughter had gone flying out the window—which is exactly what her daughter was afraid of and why she hadn't been able to tell them.

When I saw her afterward, she said, "I wish I could tell you there was something wrong with me, that I could say I had ADHD or a mental illness, but the truth is, I was being a brat. I knew that one day I'd be an adult and I'd have responsibilities, and I had this amazing opportunity to just play. I knew it would hurt my parents, but I figured I'd deal with that when it happened." And I have to say that I respected her for being so honest with me, and with herself.

This is a prime—if extreme—example of a child whose parents went over, above, sideways, and upside down to smooth every bump and give her everything, and what they created was a kid so vulnerable, entitled, and paralyzed by her own fabulousness that she was completely nonfunctioning.

Many of the teens I work with tell me they feel as if they are their parents' "project." The pressure on them always to do better or to live up to someone else's expectations is making them frantic. Not long ago I heard a story from a principal at a highly respected school that would have been funny if it weren't so sad. He told me that a mother had called him to complain that her son got only 90 percent on a project. The principal was confused and wondered why she was so upset. Ninety percent, after all, is a high mark. But the mother insisted that the project was worth much more. When the principal asked how she knew this, the mother replied that she knew it was worth more because she had a master's degree in English and had done the project herself, since her son had too much other work to do. The principal asked her if she saw any problem with this explanation, and sadly, she answered no.

The Gift of Making Their Own Mistakes

Instead of trying to cover up their mistakes, "fix" them, or prevent them from happening in the first place, what we really need to teach our kids is that mistakes are a gift from which they will learn and grow.

When I was quite young, I was a gifted pianist and played in competitions with much older children. I learned from that experience that when you're competing, if you make a mistake, you don't stop and start over. You keep on playing and hope no one will notice. Later, as a young therapist, I stuck to the same routine and quickly discovered that it was the worst thing I could have done. If you make a mistake with a client and don't admit it, you're likely to hurt her. And not only that, the more you try to pretend that the mistake didn't happen, the less competent you appear to be. Once you own the mistake, once you say, *You're right, I blew it*, or

You're right, you told me that and I forgot, you can correct the error and move on.

In her book *Mindset: The New Psychology of Success,* Carol Dweck, a professor of psychology at Stanford University, talks about a study she and her colleagues conducted with two groups of fifth-grade students over a period of ten years. One group was consistently praised for their hard work while the second group was praised for their intelligence. In an interview published in 2008 in the *Toronto Star,* Dweck reported that the second group tended to give up when the assignment was too challenging because they didn't want to look dumb, while the group who were praised for hard work "remained confident and engaged, and their performance increased fairly dramatically." In other words, those who were praised for effort rather than braininess developed the capacity to learn from their mistakes.

We need to help our kids understand that making mistakes is part of the learning process and that being comfortable with their blunders will make them more likely to stick with whatever they're doing long enough to learn to do it well. This is a particularly valuable lesson for gifted kids, whose sense of self is wrapped up in the idea that they're smarter than everyone else, and for kids who are perfectionists and tend to beat themselves up when they do something less than perfectly.

Letting our kids learn from their mistakes while also making sure they know we're holding on to the other end of the rope is one of the biggest gifts we can offer them. But again, maintaining the connection without interfering is a delicate balancing act—one that we don't seem to be handling as well as we could.

Ironically, despite all our hovering and protecting, a study conducted in the 1980s and published in *USA Today* showed that most parents spent less than seven minutes a *week* talking with their kids. If that was true then, imagine what the numbers must be like today! We're all so plugged into our electronic devices that we've become unplugged from one another. The results of another study released in 2010 by the Kaiser Family Foundation found that kids between the ages of eight and eighteen spend an average of seven hours and thirty-eight minutes on some form of electronic media—often more than one at a time. And we adults aren't much better. So, if kids are at school, or with their friends, or in their rooms most of the day and evening, and we're at work, or on the computer, or checking our BlackBerrys, how much time does that actually leave for interacting and truly connecting in a meaningful way with one another?

The Stress of Constant Communication

Our teenagers need that connection with us more than ever because their world is so driven—much more than ours was when we were growing up—by instant and constant communication with one another. All the different forms of social media, such as Facebook, Twitter, and texting make it easier for kids to reach out to their friends, it also means they're much more caught up in what's going on with their peer group—who's talking to whom, who's mad at whom, who's "in" and who's "out"—and that can be incredibly stressful. There's no time lag anymore between the moment when something happens and when someone finds out about it. Multiple conversations are being conducted simultaneously. And with so much going on, it's very difficult for kids to negotiate social situations that even adults would find problematic.

One of my teenage clients, Jill, recently met two of her camp friends for lunch, and throughout the meal the girls were "trash talking" a fourth girl, Chloe (presumably also a friend), and texting her nasty messages. Later Chloe called Jill, furious about what Jill had "said." But according to Jill she hadn't sent the messages; it had been the other girls. And now everyone was angry, texting furiously, and no one could figure out how to make things better.

Another client, Danielle, is an outgoing, popular ninth grader, and like many kids these days she had a BlackBerry, which was constantly going off. She couldn't sit through an hour-long session in my office without glancing at her phone every few minutes. And then one day she dropped it. It broke and she had to wait a week to get it replaced. When she came in that week she told me that she was actually much happier without it, and that for the first time she had time to think about things. As a result, she said she'd put herself on a techno-diet. She told her father that she didn't want another BlackBerry, but rather a regular cellphone that did nothing but phone. She also stopped looking at Facebook because she used to get upset by what she read and would feel compelled to respond immediately.

Do you remember being told that if you're angry you should sleep on it? That's a luxury teens no longer have. They're almost always responding instantly, which means they're reacting to rather than thinking about what's happening in their environment. *Not reacting impulsively* is at the core of what Connected Parenting teaches because our brain is simply incapable of responding thoughtfully when we're angry or scared. Instead of thinking before they speak (or text), many kids are thinking *after* and often regretting the words they can't take back.

All this instant communication also means that there isn't any down time. Kids don't know what to do when they have nothing to do. They don't know what it's like to be alone in the space of their own mind. Many actually get panicky. They need to be in contact and have a plan every moment of their lives. Many adolescents don't even know how to get to sleep without the television on or music playing. They don't know how to listen to the sound of silence. They've lost the ability to calm down or self-soothe. They need to be busy or connected in order to feel alive, and many sleep with their phones within easy reach. This is not to say that we adults don't also get seduced by the lure of instant communication and access to information, but because we know what it was like in the dark ages before BlackBerrys, Twitter, and Google, we're better able to tune out and give ourselves a techno-vacation.

In extreme cases—and often we see this happening to the highest functioning kids—the stress of all the frantic multiprocessing and trying to do everything at once manifests as physical illness. Kids get headaches, stomachaches, ulcers, even heart palpitations, all from the constant stress of trying to do more than is humanly possible. For these teens, being busy and needed means being important. And it may also, at least in some cases, be a way for them to avoid looking inward and confronting their own issues or demons. As parents, we need to help these superkids become more aware of their stress levels so that they can take control of the stress before it takes control of them—and becomes a pattern for life. Encouraging them to take up yoga or learn meditation to help them quiet their mind and find stillness within may be one option. And if they can't do it on their own, they may need to work with a cognitive behavioral therapist who can teach them some techniques for recognizing and managing stress.

The Need for Instant Gratification

A friend told me a funny story recently that speaks directly to the issue of constant connection. Her teenage daughter came to her brandishing the cordless telephone and insisting there was "something wrong with it." When my friend put the offending receiver to her ear, what she heard was a busy signal. Her daughter had never heard a busy signal in her life and thought it was just "dumb" that something like this could happen. My friend and I laughed when she told me the story, but it has serious implications.

The ability to wait, that is, to delay gratification, is an important component of emotional well-being and life success. In a famous experiment conducted in the 1960s by psychologist Walter Mischel, who was then at Stanford University, a group of four-year-olds were given a marshmallow and told they could have another, but only if they waited twenty minutes before eating the first one. Some could wait and others couldn't, but what's most interesting is that when the researchers followed the progress of each child into adolescence, they found that those who'd been able to wait were not only better adjusted and more dependable (according to surveys of their parents and teachers), but also scored an average of 210 points higher on the Scholastic Aptitude Test.

It's All About Them

The ability to delay gratification is related to impulse control, and is also an indication of how entitled an individual feels. We've already discussed the fact that adolescents and teens tend to be egocentric in the best of circumstances. And today, unfortunately, the combination of hovering parents, pressure to be the best, and easy access to instant gratification is creating a generation of young adults that is more narcissistic and egotistical than any in the past. A study led by Jean Twenge, a psychology professor at San Diego State University, examined the answers of 16,000 college students across the country who filled out the Narcissistic Personality Inventory between 1982 and 2006, responding to such statements as "If I ruled the world, it would be a better place" and "I think I am a special person." Twenge and her fellow researchers concluded that "young people born after 1982 are the most narcissistic generation in recent history." In fact, the average 2006 college student scored almost as high on the narcissism scale as the average celebrity from a group collected by addiction specialist Dr. Drew Pinsky.

The problem, I think, is that if an adolescent grows up believing someone will always be there to smooth the path ahead and to clean up afterward, if he lives in a world where he has instant access to almost anything his heart desires, and if, on top of that, he believes he's *got* to be the best, whatever it takes, he's in grave danger of believing he's the Sun King.

Friends and colleagues tell me all the time that many young people today lack the work ethic we were brought up with. Instead of wanting to please the boss, they believe that everything from the hours they work to the assignments they're given ought to be negotiable. They don't understand or feel the need to meet deadlines. They believe that as long as they keep texting their revised schedule to their professors or bosses, they aren't actually late for an appointment. And then, if they're criticized or corrected, they become overwhelmed and tend to fall apart.

Our goal should be to parent our children in a way that allows them to make their own choices and learn naturally from the consequences. If they've never been held accountable, they're likely to grow up into brats in adults' clothing.

Preparing Them to Launch

By the time our kids become adolescents we have a tendency to see them as our social, emotional, and intellectual equals. We think they know (or should know) everything we know, and when they behave badly we assume they know better. But they don't.

At best, adolescents are in a difficult stage—no longer children but not quite adults—and their behavior swings between these two poles. They want to be adults and make their own decisions, but at the same time they miss being kids. That's why your twelve- or thirteen-year-old daughter may be sitting in her room secretly playing with her Barbies one minute and doing something totally adult the next. They're riding an emotional rollercoaster, one minute believing that adults know everything and they'll never know as much and the next minute that adults don't know anything at all.

We tend to react to those mood swings by treating our kids as adults one minute and as babies the next. That's understandable, considering their erratic behavior, but it serves only to compound their confusion and contribute to their stress. Instead, we need to provide them with a consistent, loving, predictable environment that will allow their brain to develop and thrive. We need to be good listeners and supportive guides. Parents sometimes attempt to connect with their kids by becoming their buddies and acting as their peers, but that's not what kids want, and in the long run it's a strategy that only confuses them more. Whatever their actions and attitudes may be showing you, they don't want or need you to be their buddy. When I explain this to clients I like to use the analogy of the captain of an airplane. When you hit a patch of turbulence, you don't want the captain to be strolling down the aisle chatting up the passengers; you want him to be in the cockpit, speaking calmly over the intercom and taking control.

In the preceding chapter we talked about how kids try to push their parents away by criticizing and insulting them, which is a normal part of the separation process. If you're trying to become your kid's friend by adopting his language or dress code or style, you won't be connecting in the best, most positive way, and you'll probably embarrass him as well. Try to think of your teen's world as a foreign country: Teenland. When we visit another country we don't immediately adopt the local customs or costumes, but we do (or should) respect cultural differences. There are guides available that educate businesspeople about the manners and mores of other countries so that they won't lose a deal by inadvertently insulting their hosts. So although we need to educate our teens about what's acceptable in Adultland, to close the deal successfully we also need to understand that things are different in Teenland. We need to recognize and respect the fine line between friendship and parenting. If we can do that, we'll be preparing to launch them into the adult world with all the skills, resilience, and confidence they need to flourish.

You can't overprotect your child and then push a button when they go off to college or move out of your home and expect them to become adults overnight. In the pages that follow I'll be helping you develop the understanding and techniques you need in order to launch them most effectively. The whole point of parenting is to nurture and create independent people. If our child is in his or her mid-twenties and still dependent on us, then we haven't done our job.

THREE

Using the CALM Technique to Let Them Know You "Get" What They're About

The fact that teens are in the process of separating from you while at the same time needing to know they're still attached gives rise to many of the unpleasant or downright unacceptable behaviors they exhibit. I know, it's complicated, but if the concept is difficult for you, think how much harder it must be for your teen! It's up to us as parents to let our kids know that the attachment is there—and, if the bond has been frayed, to get it back in place.

That said, bear in mind that separation is a normal part of maturation. We want our kids to grow into adults with opinions, interests, and a peer group of friends. Not long ago a client called me desperate for advice because, as she put it, her son was a "helicopter kid." He thought of himself as a little adult and all he wanted to do was hang out with her and her friends. He was offended that the world didn't see him as the adult he considered himself to be. While she was happy that her son was so bonded to her, she knew the relationship wasn't healthy for either of them, and frankly it was sometimes annoying. I've known other kids like that—little clones of Alex P. Keaton, the Michael J. Fox character on the *Family Ties* sitcom. They may not actually wear a suit and tie and carry a briefcase, but they might as well, and it isn't any healthier for them than having a helicopter parent. Connection is all about balance, and that means establishing and maintaining appropriate boundaries.

Staying Connected in Changing Times

As Gabor Maté and Gordon Neufeld explain in their book *Hold On to Your Kids*, historically—in the olden days, as kids might say— adolescents were almost literally bonded to their parents. In fact, many cultures don't have a word or definition for adolescence; it's not a stage or a concept that's recognized. Indeed, it now appears that adolescence may be a phenomenon of Western society rather than a stage of human development. Historically, boys were apprenticed and often went to work side by side with their fathers. They wanted to prove themselves and to be accepted as men. Girls joined their mothers in the kitchen, caring for younger siblings and generally doing adult tasks. Adult women became their peers; they wanted to impress those women and prove that they could fit into the adult world. In short, teens had a clear place and sense of purpose, aspiring to become grownups and to be accepted by the adults in their community. They were apprentice adults who had jobs and responsibilities but still depended on adults to guide and teach them. They were nurtured, guided, and kept safe by adults around them until they could take care of themselves.

With the advent of the Industrial Revolution, apprenticeship was no longer the norm and mandatory education became the law. Teenagers were sent off to high school where they were surrounded by their peers, all without fully formed frontal lobes. What this meant—and still means—is that large groups of people who were not quite grown up and who still needed direction began to depend not on adults but rather on one another for guidance. And the more teens become oriented to their peers, the less they're bonded to their parents. They come to feel detached and even estranged from the important adults in their lives.

As a result we've come to believe that it's normal for an adolescent to hide in his bedroom or pretend he doesn't know us at the mall. We tend to leave him alone instead of trying to engage him or urging him to come out and be part of the family. And in time, something in his brain starts to tell him you don't love him, and he feels rejected. You've given him enough slack on the rope to let him choose to stay in his room, but without meaning to, you've given him too much slack: he can no longer feel the tension. His reaction, paradoxically, is to become unpleasant and difficult. You'd think he'd want to make himself more lovable, but that isn't the way the brain works. If he tried to *make* you love him, and you still didn't, he wouldn't be able to stand it, so instead he thinks, *Okay, if my parents don't love me, at least I'll know why*, and he behaves badly. This is a defense mechanism that can become quite pronounced in teenagers, and a behavior that is among the most challenging for parents to deal with.

Clients often ask me *why* their child started to hide out in his room to begin with. Did they do something to cause it? It's hard to know the answer, and after a while it doesn't matter. Very likely, as the adolescent's brain starts to change and he becomes more bonded to his peers, he also begins to disconnect from his parents, and one of the ways that break manifests is in his separating himself physically from you by literally shutting you out of his room. The relationship between you then deteriorates further as each of you reacts to the behavior of the other. Trying to get back to the root cause of the problem is a bit like making a fruit smoothie and then trying to pick out the strawberries. It can't be done.

What we need to understand as parents is that the teen who's spending way too much time behind that closed door is actually feeling disconnected, unprotected, and unloved. All we see is the bad behavior, and that's what we react to. We get annoyed, we yell, we ground him, or we just try to ignore him, and the cycle continues.

Looking for the Silver Lining

Instead of focusing so much on our teen's bad behavior, we need to look for the things he does well and the times he does what's asked of him. Have you ever noticed that once someone brings something to your attention—a book or a movie or how much orange everyone is wearing this spring—you suddenly notice it everywhere? Part of our brain, the reticular activating system, is responsible for filtering out the irrelevant data that comes at us all the time so that we can focus on what's important and not go mad from sensory overload. Once something is brought to our attention it comes into focus and we start to notice it more. If, for example, you get up in the morning thinking *This is going to be a bad day,* chances are that's what it'll feel like. While the day may not really be worse than any other, you'll notice all the "bad" things you wouldn't have paid attention to if your brain hadn't tagged them with that waking thought. It's like signing up to receive a Google alert every time something negative happens. In much the same way, if you're focusing on your child's bad behavior, that's what you're going to notice. He may have done five really great things on any given day, but they won't register until you start to look for them.

Maybe one of your kids is constantly telling you that you "always" take her brother's side, even though you can name a hundred times when you took her side. That isn't very different from what we do when we notice only our child's bad behavior. We may, without realizing it, be confirming her own self-definition as "bad." We also tend to talk about our kids in front of them as if they weren't listening, but they are. If we keep talking about how impossible they are, that will be the story they believe about themselves, and then they may just shrug and think, *Why even bother? It's just who I am.* We need to let them know when we notice something good, and use that as an opportunity to mirror and connect.

Change Begins with Us

This is where we get to the "now what?" part of Connected Parenting. Most parenting books tell you how important it is to listen to and validate your child's feelings, but very few tell you exactly why and how. The assumption is that we can all just do it instinctively. Unfortunately, our own feelings, worries, anger, exhaustion, or guilt often get in the way. Moreover, the act of listening deeply is a skill many therapists acquire only after years of training.

Investing in this approach to parenting is incredibly rewarding, but it isn't easy. It takes commitment, practice, and a willingness to make mistakes and forgive yourself. Because the strategies I'll be teaching are based on therapy techniques, there's really nothing to be gained by kicking yourself for not having done it before. These techniques don't come naturally to most of us, and some can even feel counterintuitive. This means that if you wait to feel like using these strategies, you'll be waiting a long time. You'll have to create new habits and build the necessary neuropathways in your own brain, which takes practice. Eventually it will come more naturally. Just remember that even our clumsy early attempts and the smallest amount of connecting on a deep level will create positive change.

We often think that if we yell at our teen and make him feel bad enough he'll make the logical decision to change his behavior, or that if we explain things rationally he'll understand. But it just doesn't work that way. When we yell at him, and even when we patiently explain what he's doing wrong, what we're really doing is letting him know that his feelings aren't valid, that he shouldn't be feeling what he's feeling. We're creating a situation in which he's concentrating on how we're making *him* feel—ashamed and/or guilty—instead of paying attention to how he's making *us* feel. In short, if we want to help our teen see that he's being rude or selfish, we need to start by changing our own reactions. If we respond with anger, yelling and listing all his faults, he'll see us as mean. Most teens don't walk away from this kind of diatribe thinking, *Wow, I can't believe I just made my dad feel that way.* They walk away thinking, *What a #@$#! He's so mean!* We've actually undermined ourselves, and our point has been lost in a storm of hurt feelings and anger.

Teens remember not what we say to them but how we make them feel when we say it, which is why yelling and tough love are often ineffective or backfire completely. Ask yourself this: If what you've been doing so far is yelling, being tough, and taking away privileges, why is it not working? The answer is that the bond between you and your teen has suffered and needs to be strengthened. You need to find a neutral and confident voice and contain behaviors in a fair and effective way. Until you're able to let your teen know that you understand what he's feeling, even though you may not approve or agree with the way he's expressing those feelings, you can't expect him to honestly reflect on his own behavior.

The way to let him know that is by mirroring. Remember that in Chapter One I explained how the mirror neuron system works and what's going on in your teenager's brain. Mirroring is a way to reflect back what another person is experiencing on an emotional level so that she *feels* heard and understood. When someone—in this case your teen—is upset, angry, or scared, she's got cortisol pumping into her system. She'll go into the fight-or-flight response, and the thinking part of her brain will shut down. She'll behave as if she were being chased by a tiger. The only way to get her to consider what you need to say is to first make her feel safe. To do that you need let her know you hear her and empathize with *her* feelings. And that has to happen on an emotional, not an intellectual level. When she feels she's been heard and understood her brain will be flooded with oxytocin, and once that happens—but not before—she'll be calm enough to listen, reflect, and consider your point of view. Until then, she remains completely invested in whatever she's trying to convey—*This is horrible! You're mean! My life is going to be ruined!*—and will keep punching away more and more frantically at the "send" button to get the message across.

So, by trying to argue with or correct behavior in a teen (or anyone for that matter) who's in fight-or-flight mode, we actually make the situation worse instead of better. It's important to underline the fact that the brain has two main systems for dealing with conflict—the adrenaline-based, impulsive fight response and the oxytocin-based response that relies on the wisdom of the frontal lobes to engage in creative problem-solving and higher-order thinking.

If we want to help our teens avoid fight-or-flight responses, we also need to control our own fight-or-flight response. If our teen is stuck in the moment we need to take a step back, calm down, and remember what we're trying to achieve. If we allow ourselves to get sucked in by her emotional state there'll simply be two of us whose thinking brain isn't working.

The goal is to change our teen's brain chemistry on an emotional level so that we can *then* speak to the thinking brain, discuss the problem as we see it, and find a solution. So we first need to *temporarily* set aside our own agenda (which is generally to correct or contain some kind of behavior) and devote ourselves completely to understanding *her* agenda so that we can then get her to listen to ours. This isn't something we instinctively *want* to do; what we want to do is get our own message across right away. Therefore, we need to be brave enough to try the opposite of what we want to do and what we think is going to work.

Staying CALM to CALM Your Teen

Mirroring is a therapeutic concept that I've broken down into steps in order to develop the CALM technique, which was outlined briefly in the Introduction to this book. It's the version of mirroring that I've developed and practice with my clients and that I'll now be teaching you to use with your teens. Using the CALM technique is the first and most important step in communicating with your teen. It must precede any correction, guidance, teaching, or imposition of consequences. The technique has a twofold purpose: to de-escalate emotions in the moment and, over the long term, to help your teen become more emotionally resilient and better able to organize and regulate his own emotions.

My first supervisor once told me, when I was having a particularly difficult time connecting with a challenging client, that it's critical to tolerate negativity and above all to show "ruthless compassion," meaning that you need to set everything else aside, including your own feelings, and concentrate on showing unrelenting understanding of what the other person is feeling. Those words have stayed with me as a way to define what I consider an important goal to strive for, not only as a therapist but also as a mother and a person.

The three-step formula is always this:

1. CALM
2. Present the problem
3. Find a solution

This is the formula you'll be using whether you're helping your teen deal with a painful issue, asking him to go to bed, dealing with the fact that she's smoking, or getting him to be nicer to his siblings. You'll need to use two to three CALMing statements before you attempt to correct or guide your teen's behavior. If he doesn't calm down after two or three statements, he's in a fight-or-flight mode, or as I call it, an emotional vortex. He'll need ten to twenty minutes to calm down on his own, after which time you can try the CALM technique again.

What I've found, both in private practice and in the seminars I teach, is that when I first begin to explain mirroring everyone nods enthusiastically. When I ask how many already mirror with their children, almost every hand goes up. But then, when we begin to role-play, it becomes immediately clear that what they're doing isn't really mirroring at all. By breaking it down into stages, the CALM technique makes mirroring accessible to every parent. As I explained in the Introduction, CALM is an acronym that stands for

Connect
Affect
Listen
Mirror

Connect

Connecting means giving your undivided attention, making eye contact, and using your body as well as your voice to match the urgency of the message your teen is trying to send. It means demonstrating that you're fully invested in the conversation. It means doing everything in your power to show your teen that you're honestly and truly trying to understand what he's thinking and feeling. When *you* feel the connection, you'll know you're doing it right and your teen will sense that you're *finally* listening to him.

What you don't want to do is calmly *interpret* what he's telling you by saying "It sounds like …" or "That must make you feel …" These are observational statements that tend to sound phony, and as though you've figured out something about him. The result is to separate rather than connect the observer and the observed. Think of it this way: if you're really angry or upset and trying to tell someone how you feel, if that person tells you to calm down or says "Gee, it sounds as if you're really angry," it's only going to make you more upset or more angry. You'll probably start screaming, "I can't calm down; don't tell me to calm down!" or "You bet I'm angry. Wouldn't you be angry?"

Nor do you want to tell stories about when a similar thing happened to you. He doesn't want to hear about your experiences, he just wants to feel that you're listening. This is about him, not you, and if you make it sound as if it's about you, he may well perceive that his own feelings are being invalidated. So, to mirror effectively, it's essential that you set your own agenda aside and devote all your energy to showing that you understand his.

Think about the people you choose to confide in or to whom you go for support. They're most likely *not* the people who launch into a lecture about how you can avoid the problem next time or who ramble on about their own experiences. Imagine that you've had a terrible day. Maybe a neighbor blasted you about something and left you rattled. Now your spouse comes home, you begin to tell him what happened, and his response is to say, "I don't know why you even engaged in a conversation with her in the first place. You should have just walked away." Or maybe he says, "Oh, she's not so bad. I've told you not to put the garbage on her side of the walk." How does that affect you? Most likely it makes you feel invalidated and leaves you wondering why you even bothered to mention it. You may notice a feeling in your stomach as if you'd been dropped or abandoned in the conversation, and you probably feel worse, not better than you did before you had that conversation.

Now think of someone you love to confide in. What he might say would be more along the lines of what I call the Best Friend Response. He'd probably lean in and say, "No way. She said what? Are you kidding me? And you're always so nice to her!" That's the kind of response that would soothe you. It would leave you feeling heard, supported, and cared for.

If we want our teens to talk to us, we need to provide them with many of those moments when they walk away feeling they've been listened to and understood. Their brain will have been flooded with those lovely reward chemicals, and they'll want to come back again and again for the comfort of feeling those chemicals at work. If, on the other hand, we're too angry or too upset when they confide in us, they'll decide that we either don't understand or can't handle their feelings.

This is particularly true when they're sad. There's nothing harder than listening to our daughter cry after being dumped by her boyfriend or listening to our son describe being picked on by a nasty peer. Part of suspending our agenda is to suspend our overwhelming desire to fix the problem or talk them out of their sadness. But when all your teen wants is for someone to understand her sadness, there's nothing less satisfying to hear than "Oh, don't worry about that guy. I'm sure you'll find someone better. Why don't you just spend more time with your girlfriends?" One of my clients once said that you have to "dare to be there," which means being able to stay in that place of hurt, anger, or sadness with your child so that she can learn she'll be okay—not by walking around, over, or under the problem, but by bravely walking through it.

Affect

The word "*affect*," used as a noun, means, in psychological terms, the outward display of feelings and emotions through nonverbal means such as facial expression, body language, and tone of voice. When you're mirroring, you're joining with your teen by reflecting his affect back to him.

Mirroring is powerful because it's more about affect than words. If you were making interpretative statements, your child would be processing those statements through the language center of his brain. When you mirror, however, you're bypassing language and connecting directly with his limbic brain. This allows him to experience the chemical reward of having his brain flooded with oxytocin. And that, in turn, has a calming effect.

To be effective it must be genuine; you must really try to put yourself in their shoes and imagine how you would feel. A friend of mine got it perfectly when she said it's the difference between admiring someone's sweater and actually trying it on. When you mirror, you're trying on your kid's sweater; you're inside it and feeling it. Instead of saying "Gee, that looks like a nice sweater!" you're saying "Oh, this sweater really feels good; it's so comfortable." There is, however, a subtle difference between allowing someone to feel that you understand what *he* feels, and starting to rave yourself. I call that hijacking the problem. It's his problem, not yours, and if you start to make it sound as if it's your problem too, he's only going to think the situation is even worse than he'd assumed. You want to reflect *his* urgency, not inject your own. You need to remain CALM in order to CALM him. In fact, staying calm is absolutely essential.

Listen

Very often we don't really listen to our kids. Instead, we more or less listen with one ear when we're in the midst of doing something else. But when you mirror, you have to give your teen your full attention. One way of letting her know you're doing this is by using her own words to convey your understanding. It's extremely important, then, that you listen intently to the words your teen is saying. There are four ways you can convey the fact that you're listening: you can *paraphrase*, you can *clarify*, you can *summarize*, and you can *wonder out loud*.

To demonstrate how each of these works, consider this scenario: you've planned a family visit to one of your cousins and your fifteen-year-old son is refusing to go. All he wants to do is stay home and play some new game he's got for his computer. Typically your dialogue would start with a statement along these lines: "I do everything for you, you're not asked to do much ... You certainly are coming with us, and you need to get off that computer anyway." To which he might answer: "You're so unfair. I just want to stay home. Your cousin is so lame and there's nothing to do there anyway." This dialogue is leading to an angry impasse.

Using the CALM technique, you could:

Paraphrase by saying something like "Oh right, I forgot you got that new game. You were so excited about buying it. Now I get why coming with us would be boring."

Or *clarify*: "So tell me about this new game. What's different about it and why is it so challenging?"

Or *summarize*: "You talk about this happening a lot. You can't do what you want because of family stuff going on and it's always so boring."

Or you can *wonder out loud* by saying something like "I'm wondering if it just feels awkward for you to spend time with so-and-so and staying home just feels easier?" If you're wrong, he'll tell you. If you're right, your observation might help start a whole new conversation that gets to the underlying problem. And if he tells you you're wrong, you can mirror that by saying something like "I'm sorry. I really blew that one," and then move on. You may find that, after taking some time to think about it and make the connection, he comes back to tell you that you were right. But even if you really were way off base, you will have demonstrated that you were trying to hear him and understand what he was going through.

The hard part is that while you're saying these things you need to remain calm and, most important, suspend your own agenda for the moment. There'll be time later, once safety is established and he's sure you're listening, to tell him why he *should* go and that he *will* go. Meanwhile you need to use your affect—your body language, your facial expressions, and your tone of voice—so that the message you convey sounds empathic rather than sarcastic. All of that doesn't necessarily come naturally—especially when what you're really thinking is *I can't believe he's carrying on like this and being so selfish. He should care about his family, especially after all I do for him, and he spends too much time on that damn computer anyway.* Getting it right can take practice.

Mirror

When you connect, use your affect to reflect your understanding, and truly listen, you're mirroring and creating a moment of deep connection.

Recently I was teaching the technique to a group of camp

counselors. One of them was playing the role of the child and I was being the counselor. As I started to mirror I could see the counselor tearing up, and she actually started to cry. We all had a great laugh about that, but something important had happened. Even though we were role-playing, my mirroring had the same effect on her brain chemistry as if the situation were real. That's how powerful it is. And remember, you're doing this to change your teen's brain chemistry so that he or she will CALM down and be able to listen to *you*. The key to mirroring successfully is to really try to be empathic. Imagine how you felt at that age, or think of a similar situation you've experienced. The more genuine your response, the more moving and effective the interaction will be.

If your teen rejects your attempt to CALM him, stay neutral and don't appear offended. Just say something like, "You know, I've been thinking about how I often don't really listen to you and I'm really working on it. I guess I still have a way to go." Then walk away. Most likely he'll reflect on that and evaluate his own behavior, and it may go very differently the next time.

This technique will not come easily. It requires you to always take a moment to consider whether you're about to say something to your teen that you feel like saying or something that you think he needs to hear. This is the difference between reacting and responding. It's also a great way to demonstrate that it's possible to think before you speak. If *we* can't do that, how can we expect them to do it?

Many people find that the hardest part of mirroring is simply staying in the moment. You have to overcome the urge to solve, fix, or correct the problem until you've truly listened. Don't worry about how you've handled this in the past, and don't worry if you make mistakes and blow it. You can always go back and repair the damage (see page 68). Remember, too, that this is a counterintuitive technique, meaning that you won't feel like using it. You'll feel like reprimanding, yelling, or even cheerleading.

Transforming No-Win Encounters

Here are two classic no-win encounters that will be familiar to many parents. Let's see how they typically play out, and how they might go differently if you mirror.

Your daughter needs to get to school and she's having a meltdown because she's UGLY! She knows she looks absolutely hideous. Your instinct, of course, is to say "But honey, you look fine," first because she really does look fine and second because you're her mother and even if she looked terrible you'd still tell her she looks fine. But saying that is only going to lead to further screaming—"You have to say that. You're my mother!"—although probably with a few insults thrown in: "What do you know anyway? You're a hundred and eight years old and you have no idea what's cool!"

So what are you supposed to do? Tell her she's right and she looks ugly? Just ignore the fact that you were trying to help and she took a nasty dig at you? No! What you're supposed to do is let her know that you understand what she's feeling, even though you don't see it that way, and then, when the time is right, let her know the dig was not okay. So your response might go, "Probably you don't even want to hear what I have to say because you know I'm going to say you look great. But right now you can't stand the way you look. When you look in the mirror all you see is that you look horrible." You're not saying that *you* think she looks horrible; you're just trying on the sweater and imagining what you'd feel if you were in her place.

I know that with every ounce of your being you want to assure your daughter that she looks fine, or that she needs to get over it, but the more you offer that assurance or dismiss her feelings, the more invested she'll become in delivering the message (that she's UGLY!) you've clearly not received, and the screaming, ranting, and hysterics will escalate. But once she knows the message has been delivered, she can stop waving it in front of your face and start to calm down.

Here's another situation most parents have found themselves in—probably more than once. Your teen wants to go to a party that *all the other kids* are going to, but for whatever reason (it's too far away or you don't believe an adult will be present), you don't want him to go. He's already hysterical and screaming because he'll be the *only one* not there and he's going to be a social outcast. He might even have to move to Alaska.

Remembering to match his affect and urgency, you might start by saying something like, "So ..." ("so" is usually a good way to start), "let me understand this. For you, if you can't go to the party you don't see how you're going to get past it. This is it. You feel as if socially it'll be all over for you." Those are clarifying statements that show him you're really trying to understand how bad this is for him. And you need to show him with your body language and the intensity of your expression that you're working hard to get it right.

But you need to do this without using any interpretive language, such as "It seems to me ..." or "You sound like ..." You must also be careful not to sound sarcastic. Keep that "You have got to be kidding me!" tone out of your voice. And you don't want to inject yourself into the problem by saying, "I know how you feel because the same thing happened to me. But I survived it and so will you." First, this isn't about you, and second, he couldn't care less about what happened to you back in the dark ages when you were a teen and probably a really nerdy one, too. Nor should you remind him of the party he went to last week or all the parties you've let him go to this year or tell him for the thousandth time that we can't always have what we want. There'll be time later on to deliver those messages, and ways to deliver them so that they can be heard, accepted, and understood.

At the moment, if he thinks you're not getting the real message—which is that if he can't go to this party he'll be a total social outcast for the rest of high school—he's just going to send it louder and louder, as if you were a foreigner and repeating the same words at amplified volume will miraculously make you understand. "You just don't get it! They probably didn't even *have* parties when you were my age. And if they did you probably never got invited anyway!" It can get pretty brutal.

But if you continue to try to understand ("Help me get this …") and summarize ("This is tough for you. These parties are huge …"), he'll start to de-escalate. He probably won't embrace you for refusing to let him go, but he will calm down and get over it, probably more quickly than you anticipated. You can empathize, listen well, and still say no. What you say is often not as important as how you say it.

When you're CALMing your teen, you're acting more or less as the therapist talking a jumper down off the ledge. Admittedly, that's a lot easier to do when the source of the problem is something a friend or a teacher did rather than something you're doing. But it is effective in all situations. In fact, I believe it's the only way to de-escalate a situation in which you're the perceived bad guy without allowing it to erupt into World War III.

Here's another scenario. This time I'm going to put both parties' thoughts in parentheses like cartoon thought bubbles. Once again the first example demonstrates how the conversation would typically go if both parent and child reacted instinctively, and the second shows how it might proceed using the CALM technique.

Let's say you're trying to get your four-year-old son dressed and ready for day care when teenage Maggie comes in screaming, "MOM! Where's my blue top? I want to wear it today …" (*Oh my god, I have to look good today or Miranda will say something horrible to me. I need that shirt. I look hideous in everything else. My whole day will suck … WHERE IS IT?*)

You barely look up when you say, "It's in the dirty laundry basket." (*Great! Here we go again. Why is she always asking me where her things are? She should know where they are. Why do I always have to be the one to think of everything? Why won't this kid put his LEG IN HIS PANTS? We're late ... ARGH!*)

"I NEED IT! I NEED TO WEAR IT TODAY!" (*She never ever listens to me. She's always busy with that little kid. I need her too sometimes. My life is over if I don't have that shirt.*) "MOM!"

"WHAT? WILL YOU CUT IT OUT! I'm trying to get your brother dressed. You're fourteen years old. You shouldn't need me to keep track of your clothes. I told you the top was in the laundry, so you'll have to wear something else!" (*Unbelievable! I have to do everything around here. When is she going to start doing something for herself?*)

"I DON'T WANT TO WEAR ANYTHING ELSE. I WANT THAT SHIRT! YOU SAID YOU WOULD WASH IT! I HATE YOU! YOU NEVER CARE ABOUT ME!" (*She doesn't care about me at all. Why can't my stupid brother get himself dressed? I'm going to have the worst day and she doesn't care at all!*)

So now everyone is in fight-or-flight mode, and it's not hard to see how this will play out. Now let's see how differently it would go if Maggie's mother had used the CALM technique.

Maggie comes in screaming, "MOM! Where's my blue top? I want to wear it today." (*Oh my god, I have to look good today or Miranda will say something horrible to me. I need that shirt. I look hideous in everything else. My whole day will suck. WHERE IS IT?*)

(*Great! Here we go again. Why is she always asking me where things are? She should know where they are. Why do I always have to be the one to think of everything? Why won't this kid put his LEG IN HIS PANTS? We're late ... ARGH!*) You're about to yell back "It's in the laundry basket!" when you stop and think, *Okay, I could yell at her to go find it herself, but this is the hundredth time we've had this conversation so it's time for a new approach.* This is where you postpone introducing your agenda. There'll be time to discuss her tone of voice after you get her CALMed.

"You mean that stunning blue one you just bought?"

"Yeah! That one. WHERE IS IT?"

"You're not going to like this because it sounds like your whole outfit depends on that shirt, but it's still in the laundry."

"MOM, that sucks! I put it in there days ago!"

"It would look amazing with those pants. They look perfect together!" And now you can start to introduce your agenda: "I don't love the way you're talking to me, but I get how upset you are. That outfit is fantastic!"

At this point Maggie will most likely be starting to calm down because you're empathizing with her. "What am I going to do? I have nothing else to wear!"

Don't say what you're probably thinking, which would be *Of course you do! You have more clothes than an A-list celebrity.* What you need to say instead is something like "It sucks to have the perfect outfit picked out and not be able to wear it." Then follow up with a message of competence: "I know you can do this. Give yourself a minute to think and pull something else together. You have great fashion sense. You'll come up with something terrific."

At this point, leave her alone. You've done your listening, and 85 to 90 percent of the time she'll settle down and you'll be able to move on. Later in the day or that evening you can let her know that it's not okay to use a rude tone with you and help her find a way to stay calm in the first place.

If You Get It Wrong, You Can Always Redo It

One of the wonderful things about this technique is that when you blow it you can always go back and do it over. And you *will* blow it. We all do. I've been teaching it for years and I still blow it with my own kids. So let's go back to the situation with Maggie and her blue top.

By the end of the first scenario, where the CALM technique was *not* used, Maggie would be in full meltdown mode, screaming about how if she can't wear that top she just won't go to school at all. You would also be in fight-or-flight mode, and the whole day would be off to a horrible start. You know it would have helped to CALM her, but now it's too late. That's okay because later in the day, when things have settled down, you can go back and fix it. You can say something like, "You know, when you were so upset about your blue top this morning and I said you'd just have to wear something else, and we went back and forth yelling, I didn't stop to think about what it felt like for you to have planned your entire outfit around that top only to find out you couldn't wear it. If I'd planned my whole work outfit and then discovered a piece of it was dirty I'd have had a hard time with that, too. I didn't actually think about what that was like for you."

When you're learning this technique you'll probably be doing a lot more repairing than mirroring. You'll be walking away from situations thinking, *That's not what I should have said* or *I didn't do that right*. You can always go back and say, "You know, that didn't come out the way I wanted it to. I was really trying to let you know how much I wanted to understand what you were feeling." And that's all you need to say. I assure you that just those few words will resonate powerfully with your teen.

The great thing about using the CALM technique to make repairs is that you have time to think about what you're going to say. When you're using the technique in the moment you're doing a lot of things at once: looking at your child's body language and trying to work out what it means; figuring out the intent of what she's saying; deciding how to empathize with that. It's a lot of work for the brain to do on the fly, so to speak. But with repair-mirroring you can take the time to really think about what you would have felt in her situation at that age and how you would have felt if your parent had responded the way you did. You can even practice what you're going to say out loud beforehand.

In the beginning you may not be getting the mirroring technique exactly right and your teen might "catch you" doing it. If he looks at you and says "Why are you repeating everything I'm saying?" the answer you can have ready is "Because I'm trying to be a better listener. Clearly I'm not great at it and I'm trying to get better." Most kids will walk away thinking, Okay, maybe Mom really is trying to understand me.

Putting Yourself in Their Shoes

One significant impediment to any kind of communication is that each of us is locked inside our own head and may be seeing things only from our own perspective. The key to using the CALM technique successfully is to get out of your head and inside your teen's.

The term "intersubjectivity" is used in psychoanalysis to mean that two people communicating with each other are in agreement on a specific set of meanings or the nature of a given situation. The type of therapy I practice is based on self-psychology, which assumes that the therapist and client may not necessarily be in agreement about the meaning or circumstances of a given situation and that the therapist must, therefore, be aware of the client's feelings and experiences and be prepared to look at things from the client's point of view. These are the same therapeutic skills parents need when mirroring and connecting with a teen—and that we all need when we're communicating with another person.

We all bring our own experiences and history along with us, and without our being aware of it, our past colors our perceptions in the present. Let's say you believed as a child that you needed to be the "good" kid who didn't make trouble. You may have believed this because you had a sibling who was a troublemaker or one who was sick, and you didn't want to upset your parents any more than they already were. Or perhaps you felt ignored. The beliefs that are imprinted in early childhood help determine the way our brain circuitry develops and the way we interpret the world. They are the stories we tell ourselves about who we are. They are our "theme songs." They affect our present-day relationships and underlie our arguments and differences of opinion. We tend to assume that other people come to situations and circumstances with a mindset similar to our own, when more often than not they don't. As parents, we need to be aware of how we sound to our children and how *they* perceive what we're saying. How we perceive ourselves sounding in our own head very rarely matches how it's perceived by another person. And how we perceive what our teen is trying to communicate may be quite different from how she perceives it herself. That disconnect may be compounded by the fact that teens in general aren't necessarily adept at articulating their feelings.

If we can figure out what memories drive our reactions, and the behaviors or situations that tend to upset us, we can become better able to examine our own perspective and not take personally what other people (particularly our children) say and do. We can also become better able to set aside our own agenda and really listen to our kids.

I am very aware of my own theme song. Ever since I was a little girl I've worried that people will be upset with me. Now, if I get a phone message from a client saying "Please call me as soon as you can, it's very important," my tendency is to assume I've done something wrong and to stress about why the client is upset. I can get very worked up about this, even though the "urgent" matter often turns out to be that the client needs to change an appointment. My theme song still plays, but now that I'm aware of it, I can control the volume. Being aware of your theme song and of how and when it plays will help you appreciate the fact that your teen probably sees the issue you're arguing about very differently from the way you see it.

Teens Send Messages in Many Different Ways

Teens are good at letting you know they're upset, but they don't always do it with words. Sometimes they just stomp around or slam doors or give you the silent treatment. Boys in particular may have a hard time verbalizing their feelings, perhaps because they're so overwhelmed that their brain literally shuts down, or because something is so upsetting that they don't even want to admit it to themselves.

Boys are often less verbal than girls and have a harder time talking about their feelings (which is also true of grownup boys and girls). Or they may actually have a difficult time connecting the physical sensation of an emotion to its cause. So if you ask them "What's wrong?" they may just shut down, saying "I don't know! Stop it! Just leave me alone!" It may be that they *can't* tell you, not that they don't want to. And the more you ask them the more anxious they get. They might feel the jitteriness and stomachache that come with anxiety but not understand what it means. Because traumatic or upsetting messages are stored in the feeling part of the brain, very often people have a strong physical reaction to things without necessarily being aware of what triggered it. By using the CALM technique consistently you can help your teen make those connections, gain awareness, and ultimately self-soothe.

Clients often ask me how they can possibly mirror with someone who isn't talking. Well, the time when a kid can't or won't talk may be the most important time of all for you to mirror. Teens are always communicating. By rolling their eyes or turning their back on you they're clearly saying that they're angry, you should go away, and there's no point trying to talk to you. You can mirror those messages by verbalizing what you imagine they must be thinking and reflecting their body language as if it were spoken. For example, you might say, "You just looked away from me, so clearly you're still really mad at me about ..." Sometimes you can actually help them connect things they can't put together for themselves, such as, "I'm wondering if what you're feeling is anxiety because your sister got into university and you're thinking maybe you won't, and that's why you got so upset about her borrowing your ..." Often they'll say something like "Oh, yeah," and you can see the light go on. Sometimes it won't happen in that moment, but they'll go away, the thought will percolate, and then they'll get it.

When You Don't Want to Do It Is Just When You Should

The times when your teen is yelling, acting like a drama queen, or doing something totally unacceptable are probably *not* the times you want to empathize with her feelings. Most likely it'll be the last thing you feel like doing. But that's exactly the time when you most need to do it. Just remember that you're doing it for a reason, which is to get your teen to the point where he can actually listen to you and accept what you want to teach him. If you want him to hear you, you first have to let him know that you've heard *him*. The point is not that you want him to feel good about behaving badly; the point is that it works.

It works with everyone, not just kids, because everyone wants to feel heard. This was brought home to me years ago when I was still working as a social worker within the school system. There was very little parking space at one of the inner-city schools where I worked, so to avoid blocking one another in we were constantly negotiating to determine who was going to leave first. One day when I arrived the only parking space was behind the car belonging to the French teacher. She told me she had a dentist's appointment at eleven-thirty and needed to leave by eleven. I told her that wouldn't be a problem because I was scheduled to lead a group session at another school at eleven. As it turned out, though, when I got to the office I was told that a student at another school was saying he had a gun in his backpack and wouldn't talk to anyone but me. The entire school was on lockdown, and in minutes I found myself talking to him on one phone with the principal talking to me on another and emergency services on a third. I was in the middle of all this when, at eleven o'clock, I heard myself being paged. There really wasn't anything I could do at that moment, but luckily the crisis with the student was resolved within the next fifteen minutes.

I hurried down to the parking area where the French teacher was pacing around, furious. She had curly hair, and honestly it was as if every hair on her head were standing on end. She was beside herself. As soon as she saw me she started to scream: "Who do you think you are? I told you I had an appointment! How dare you! Do you think you're the only person around here with places to go?" My natural instinct was to yell back something like "What did you want me to do? Hang up on the kid who was threatening to shoot up his entire school? Tell him to just hold that thought for a minute because I have a car to move?" But I didn't. Instead I pulled myself together and said, "You're absolutely right. You made a specific point of telling me you had to leave by eleven and I promised I'd be out of here, and then you came out and my car was still here and you paged me fifteen minutes ago and it's still here …" I matched her affect and reflected back the urgency of her message. I could tell she was trying really hard to stay mad, but she couldn't. By correctly echoing her feelings I had defused her rage. My mirroring had the effect of first bathing her brain in oxytocin, and then giving her nothing to push back against. She finally just got in her car and drove away.

Afterward I thought, *Well, that was stressful,* but the truth is, if I'd gotten into a huge fight with her it would have been even more stressful, and I'd still be going over and over the whole conversation in my head.

Of course, when I got to school the next morning, who was the first person I ran into? The French teacher. At that point I thought, *Oh great, now she's going to yell at me all over again.* But instead she came up to me and said, "You know, I have to apologize to you. I couldn't stop thinking about our conversation. You were so understanding and so kind and I was so awful to you. I couldn't sleep all night. I just felt horrible."

That's what's so powerful about this technique. Nothing I could have said to defend or justify myself in the parking lot would have brought her to that place. If I'd said "I understand that must make you very angry," she would have blown her top. If I'd said "You know, there's a very good reason why I couldn't move my car. If you'd just listen …" she probably would have said something like, "Frankly, I don't care what the reason is. You knew I had an appointment …"

The CALM technique changes people's behavior for the right reasons: for internal reasons, not out of fear or resentment but because they're able to walk away reflecting on their own behavior, not yours.

To Be CALM Is to Be More Flexible

Many parents complain to me that their kids are so oppositional and inflexible they don't even *want* to connect with them. It's natural to want to pull back and protect yourself, and it can feel unnatural to try to connect with someone who's so obviously pushing you away. But the more difficult and oppositional they are, the more you need to connect. If you can't bring yourself to try the CALM approach for the sake of your teen, then think about doing it for your own sake, because it will change your life for the better.

A part of the brain called the cingulate system runs between the two frontal lobes and is responsible for flexibility and adaptability—the ability to shift attention, to move from one idea to another, to consider your options. It's the gear-shifter that lets you know you need to stop doing one thing and start doing something else. When you're driving down the highway, for example, and another driver cuts you off, you probably think *You jerk*, and then return your attention to the road. People with cingulate problems, however, think *You jerk, you jerk, you jerk* over and over because they can't let go of the thought.

According to Daniel Amen, "The more organized the limbic system is, the easier it is for the cingulate system to shift and flow with events." So it's important to establish the emotional bond that will calm your teen so that she's better able to let go of her single-minded point of view and listen to yours. It's also why, as a parent, you need to put your own agenda aside and listen to your teen's before you can move on with your own.

Connecting Before Correcting

One mother I know was totally at odds with her adolescent daughter, Leah. Nothing Leah's mother did was ever right, and no matter what she said, Leah's answer was rude and sarcastic. Her tone of voice was so grating that more often than not her mother would respond in kind, and before they knew it they were in the middle of another stupid argument about nothing.

One day Leah returned home with her friends after having been in the sun all afternoon. It was painfully obvious that she'd forgotten to use her sunscreen. Her mother took one look at her and exclaimed, "Leah, why didn't you use your sunscreen? Your face looks like a lobster!" It was a typical mother's comment, but Leah's response was also typical: "Gee, Mom, thanks for stating the obvious!" And with that she pushed her mother on the arm and walked away in a huff, with her mother screaming, "Just a minute young lady. You come back here … Don't you dare speak to me that way!"

When Leah's mother related the incident to me, she said she'd felt hurt and embarrassed. She hadn't expected her daughter to react so violently. I explained that Leah had no doubt been painfully aware of what she looked like and that she too had been embarrassed when her mother brought it up in front of her friends.

Teenage girls tend to be incredibly focused on their appearance. Anything from having a bad hair day to not being able to find a particular piece of clothing can send them into hysterics. It has to do with raging hormones combined with the inability to step back and get some perspective (that developing frontal lobe again). Teens, and girls in particular, have trouble understanding that everyone in the world isn't always staring at them. When an adolescent girl complains that her bangs look awful, telling her that her bangs look *perfectly fine!* is only going to escalate the problem. She *knows* her bangs look *absolutely hideous* (those ANTS again), and she's just going to keep on sending that message until you understand that her life is *absolutely ruined.* If you want to get through to her you need to match her affect and mirror what she's feeling.

That will allow her to calm down enough to get out the blow-dryer and do something about fixing the problem. As a parent, you need to try to put yourself in your teenager's shoes by thinking of a situation in which you might feel equally upset. That can be difficult, especially if you're in a hurry, you need to get going, and this is her fifth meltdown today.

If you've been using the CALM technique and it's not working, it's because your teen is caught up in a vortex of emotion—and the best thing you can do is step away. Simply say, "You know, I can't talk to you right now because it's obvious that my presence isn't helping you. So I'm going to walk away and leave you to figure out what you're going to do." Follow that with a strong message of competence, such as "I know you can do it, and I know you're going to be okay." Usually she'll keep on screaming and throwing things around in her room. Just let her be. She needs a safe place to get out all those emotions. So, unless you hear breaking glass or something else that sounds really dangerous, stay away for fifteen or twenty minutes until it sounds as if calm has been restored. *Then* you can go back in and say, "How are you doing?" Of course, seeing your face may just set her off all over again. When a kid is in fight-or-flight mode (which is what that vortex is all about), her brain organizes around whatever is upsetting her. That might be the computer that's freezing up, or it could be you. If it's you, your face becomes a visual stimulus, which is why you need to remove it from her sight. You may have to repeat the whole routine. Even when you're not the cause (such as when your daughter is flinging herself around on the bed and screaming that her hair is disgusting), you still may need to remove yourself and give your teen the dignity of some privacy.

Afterward you can say, "You know, your brain gets into these vortexes and it's really hard in the moment for you to realize that it's not such a big deal ..." Or, if you need to correct behavior and impose a consequence, you can do that too. You just can't do it in the moment when she's freaking out. And the more you use the CALM technique, the more you'll be building resilience and helping her recognize when her emotional brain is taking over and shutting down her more rational brain, or frontal lobes. More and more often—but not always—she'll be able to catch herself and pull back before she goes off the deep end.

So what I explained to Leah's mom was that when Leah pushed her, a more effective response would have been to take her aside and mirror her feelings by saying something like, "Oh, Leah, I can't believe I did that. I totally embarrassed you in front of your friends. I've mortified you. Obviously you knew your face was red and that people were looking at you, and I certainly didn't need to point it out like that."

At first she looked at me as if I were out of my mind. Why would she want to empathize with someone who was so consistently rude and disrespectful? Of course I understood her reaction, but I explained that, at least at first, she needed to do it because it was what her daughter needed. She also needed to do it for herself, to mend the bond between them. I told her now that afterward, when things had calmed down and Leah was actually capable of hearing her, she could explain why the behavior was unacceptable and, if necessary, impose a consequence. Mirroring, I said, didn't mean that she was condoning the behavior, only that she understood the feelings that triggered it.

So she tried it. The very next day she came to me totally amazed. She couldn't believe it. Leah's expression had changed completely and she'd actually hugged her mother. Within a few days her mood and body language had shifted, not only with her mother but also with her friends. The true magic of this technique is that it affects your child's ability to regulate mood and interact with *all* people.

Leah is a pretty typical teen, but Jordan was a kid with more serious behavioral problems. He had frequent, violent rages during which he'd actually smash things in the house. His mother was afraid of his rages but also afraid that no one else would understand her son. As a result, she had never held him accountable or made him hold himself accountable for his behavior. He'd never learned to self-regulate because she'd never set limits or imposed consequences for what he did. Instead she thought and talked about him as if he were a severely disabled person, which is how he'd come to think of himself.

By the time I met him, Jordan was sixteen and had left school. He was so anxiety-ridden that he'd completely stopped participating in the world. He wouldn't even leave his room. His mother was now carrying food upstairs on a tray and leaving it outside his door.

I told her that the first thing on her agenda would be to re-establish a connection with her son. She started by talking to him through the door: "I'm just leaving this food outside your door. I'm not going to ask you anything. I'm not going to say anything to you. I just want you to know I'm here." After she did this a few times, still through the door, he'd ask her a question like "Do you have any juice?" The fact that she'd been leaving so quickly had given him permission to not want her there, and as a result he suddenly did want her. So when he asked if she had any juice—or cookies, or whatever—she'd just say "Yup. I'll go get them." Or "I'm not sure, I'll go check." Finally, one day he said, "Wait, where are you going?" and they had a little chat through the crack in the door. It took only a few weeks before he let her in. If he started to complain about something, she would mirror and then walk away. She was giving him the experience of that connecting moment and then leaving while he was still enjoying it; in this way, his brain would remember that moment. Within a couple of weeks Jordan came out of his room. Then he started working a few days a week with his father in his construction business.

His mother first noticed the mirroring having an effect when Jordan was sitting in the living room drinking a Coke. He'd placed the glass next to him on the sofa, and when his mother came into the room her instinct was to screech something like "Jordan, what are you doing? You've got your Coke on my leather couch and it's going to spill all over the place!" To which he would have responded by yelling at her to just leave him alone for once. But this time she stopped herself and said, "You know what, you look so comfortable, and I totally get it. Your Coke is right next to you. It's so much easier than having to lean forward and put the glass on the table. I'm trying to see it from your perspective, but here's the problem …" She hadn't gotten further than that when he said "Sorry, Mom, I'll use the coffee table" and leaned forward to put the glass on the table. To say she was in shock is putting it mildly.

The next time she noticed the mirroring effect was when Jordan came home after work with mud all over his boots. Instead of tracking the mud on the hall carpet he made a point of walking around it on the wood floor all the way to the kitchen. Instead of screaming about the muddy boots, she said "Jordan, you know what, I noticed that you took the time to walk all the way around the rug. There's not one speck of dirt on it. The floor can be washed but the rug is much harder to clean, and I just wanted to let you know that I noticed that." To which he responded, "You know, Mom, I really should have just taken my boots off. I messed up your floor, and I should have cleaned it up. I'm sorry. I'll take my boots off next time." Again, she was amazed. Jordan's mom has since gone on to start her own organization whose mission is to get the mirroring message across to other parents of kids with behavioral problems.

Jordan still has rages, but they're now much fewer and far between. And yes, this particular kid has multiple neurological problems, but the point is that if these techniques can work for someone like him, they'll certainly help your more typical, if annoying and oppositional, teen.

Creating Connecting Moments

Gabor Maté once said that we wouldn't buy a plant, put it on the windowsill, and then start screaming at it to make it grow. But too often that's what we do with our kids. Our kids are flowers, and they need nurturing as much as a plant needs water.

Mirroring is emotional nutrition for your teen's brain, but people (including me) don't always remember to do it, especially when their teen is behaving well and they have nothing to correct. But you don't have to wait for your teen to do or say something wrong in order to have an opportunity to mirror. In fact, it's the mirroring you do when things are going well—the incidental mirroring—that will gradually reduce the number of times you have to mirror in order to correct. Incidental mirroring creates connecting moments that keep your teen bonded to you so that she's less likely to act in ways she knows will upset you. Howard Glasser uses a similar technique, called active recognition, in his wonderful book *Transforming the Difficult Child*. He notes that "being noticed or recognized is more powerful than one may imagine."

If you respond in a way that lets your teen know you're really paying attention, his brain will be bathed in oxytocin and he'll feel good—about himself and about you. So, if he is telling you about something that happened at school that day, instead of saying "Oh, that's nice" and going about your business, try giving him your full attention and saying something like "Wow, are you serious? Your teacher just ignored you when you asked her a question?" Or if he's looking for something in the fridge and is upset that it's not there, you could say "Oh, I really hate it when I know exactly what I want to eat and it's not there." Then walk away and leave him with that small but powerful moment of being understood.

It doesn't have to be a long conversation. Just a little connecting moment is enough for both of you to feel the rush of oxytocin. When you have that feeling, you'll know you're doing it right—and you'll know your teen is feeling it too. He'll want more of it because it feels so good, and as a result he'll be more likely to come to you more often, to talk to you more, and to tell you when he's upset. Think of it as making healthy deposits into an emotional bank account: the more deposits you make, the stronger your bond will be. You'll even be able to blow it, get upset, and not mirror a few times, because your account will be full enough to withstand a few withdrawals. It's those moments that strengthen the bond between you that will enable you to become his "true North."

When the Bond Is Frayed

Some parents tell me that because their teens have pulled away and shut themselves off, they don't *want* to connect and the parents are reluctant even to try. My answer is that if your teen has pulled away, connecting is how you're going to get him back. In fact, I actually prescribe the technique: to CALM with your teen for ten or fifteen minutes a day as a kind of bonding medicine.

The big surly boy or snotty adolescent girl now living in your house was once your baby—and one of the most effective ways to mend your bond is to remind you both of that fact. For younger children, I call this connecting play. You can think of it as a deep connecting moment. It's one of the most powerful strategies available for making that all-important repair.

When I first read about what Daniel Amen calls "deep limbic bonding" I was truly excited, because this was something I'd been prescribing to clients for years. I knew it worked, but for a long time I didn't have the information about brain chemistry to understand on a scientific level *why* it worked. In fact, creating these deep connecting moments is mirroring in its most basic form, because it's recreating what you did instinctively when the child really was a baby—looking into her eyes, touching her face, tickling her, using a baby voice. I'm not suggesting this as a way to treat your child all the time—far from it. It's a way to create a special moment that allows you to wash both your brains in oxytocin so that you feel the bond on the deepest emotional level, which will have a lasting effect. In fact, this seems to be the fastest and most effective way to increase those reward chemicals and raise oxytocin levels. Many parents report that connecting play alone improves the relationship and decreases oppositional behavior.

You're probably thinking that your teenager would be horrified by an overt display of affection, and I certainly wouldn't recommend you do it in front of her friends. But you'll be pleasantly surprised if you try it. An overwhelming number of parents tell me that it's been incredibly helpful. Remember that your initial mirroring was helping your baby develop neuropathways, and that it's something the brain actually craves. That craving doesn't go away just because your child is older. On the contrary, those deep connecting moments take your teen back to the safety of babyhood and therefore bring down her anxiety level dramatically. If you think about it, loving couples often have special baby names they use with each other, and I believe that, subconsciously, their intimate baby talk is a way to stimulate bonding.

In *Connected Parenting* I told a story about baby play that's even more relevant here. I was doing a two-day workshop in a small private school, and was in the midst of explaining the power of baby play when one of the teachers laughed out loud. I asked her why she found it so funny, and she explained that her fourteen-year-old son was a Goth and that they'd been fighting for years. She said he would "puke on her" if she ever treated him in that manner. So I challenged her to go home and try it in a playful way. After all, if they'd been fighting for years, she had nothing to lose.

She accepted my challenge, and when I saw her the next morning the expression on her face said it all. She explained that when she'd arrived home her son was in his usual position splayed out on the sofa. Through gritted teeth she called out playfully, "Where's my little fourteen-year-old? I don't care if you're a Goth; you're the cutest little Goth I've ever seen!" And she started to tickle him. She almost fell over when, instead of "puking on her" as she'd anticipated, he threw his feet in the air and they wrestled around and had a wonderful, warm moment, after which, without having to say anything, they both knew the game was over and she went into the kitchen to start dinner.

Later that evening, as she walked past her son's bedroom door, she stopped as she always did to say goodnight to him. Without any prompting he called out in a playful baby voice, "Mommy, will you tuck me in?" They had another wonderful moment, and she said that after she left his room and closed the door behind her she slid down the wall and sat on the floor crying for all the time she'd wasted tiptoeing around the house and trying to stay out of her son's way when she could have been connecting with him. It marked the beginning of a huge, positive change in their relationship.

That teacher really threw herself wholeheartedly into my challenge and her son responded in kind, but not every child will be comfortable with that degree of physical cuddling. If your teen lets you know by his reaction that he isn't quite ready to be play-wrestling with you, you can still get out his baby pictures, videos, or a toy you might have saved. Tell him stories about things he did when he was a child. Make the connection in whatever way feels right for you and your teen, and watch his eyes light up.

Depending on how frayed the bond has become, you may be reluctant even to try this approach. If that's the case, just remind yourself what a pain you probably were as a teenager and how your own parents must have felt about you. Remember all the good moments you've had with your teen. The things that are driving you crazy are probably the things you'd miss most if anything ever happened to her. Notice and point out the traits you love about your teen. Leave her little notes. Find a baby picture and put it on her pillow. Send her funny texts. Tell her stories about when she was small. Make her feel loved and delicious. Your teen may roll her eyes and look annoyed, but I promise you that deep down somewhere she loves it and craves it.

If she rejects it from you, be a bit more subtle and look for little clues that indicate the bond is being repaired. Be prepared to take your time and let it build. Don't look hurt and walk away in a huff; she'll just think, *Well, that was pretty nasty* and feel that her behavior was justified. Simply say something like "Okay, I guess that's a little much. I'll respect you and back off." When you remain neutral, after you walk away she may begin to reflect on what happened and feel bad. The next time she may not jerk away as fast or she may stay in the room a little longer. When that happens, fight the urge to say "Isn't this great? We're having such a nice moment!" That would only send her running out of the room. Being positive but fairly neutral is what will keep her coming back.

There are lots of ways to create these powerful moments, and the more often they occur, the more rewarding they become. Even if you and your teen are already close, these connecting encounters are a wonderful way to nurture the bond between you.

A Frayed Bond Endangers
the Whole Family

Parenting and money seem to be the two issues that put the most stress on a marriage, and this is particularly true when there's a child with behavioral issues involved. We tend to manifest who we are as people in the way we parent our kids. When a child is acting out, parents often become polarized. One may take on the "hard parenting," acting as the disciplinarian and rule enforcer, while the other does the "soft parenting," the cuddling, nurturing, and generally more permissive role. Naturally, the child gravitates to the soft parent. And this polarizing can be particularly acute when there's a teenager in the mix. Teens are really good at playing one parent off against the other. And since the issues are generally about safety, the stakes are higher than when you were debating whether your five-year-old could have a cookie before dinner.

Polarizing can set in motion a destructive cycle that affects the entire family. Let's say the disciplinarian is the mother, and consequently the teen goes to her father for everything. At some point the dad decides his wife is being "too hard on the kid." He softens up more and the family is triangulated. Mom begins to feel shut out and resentful of her husband for not doing his share of the hard parenting. While the father and daughter grow closer, the mother becomes increasingly isolated. She feels disrespected and is in danger of turning into the stereotypical nagging, complaining mom.

In other variations on this dynamic, one parent may begin to protect the child he or she perceives the other parent is too hard on, or the parents may be united and the children are the ones who feel left out. The key is for both parents to be hyper-aware of what they're bringing to the situation and to find a balance. Parents need to be on the same page. The lenient one needs to step up and take on more of the hard parenting while the natural disciplinarian needs to become more nurturing. In order for this to work, each must trust the other to make the necessary alterations. In the end, we can't really change anyone but ourselves—but once we do begin to change, we'll also change the way our kids relate to us.

I don't remember who said this, but it's a wonderful analogy: being in a family is like sleeping in a water bed. When one person moves, everyone feels the ripple. A family is a system, and every member's behavior affects everyone else.

I worked with one couple whose teenage daughter, Jillian, was in their words "impossible." She was bright and functioned perfectly, except when she was at home. Although other parents thought Jillian was great, her parents thought she was a demon. Both parents were strict, but her mother was the main "enforcer" while her father acted the role of wounded dog. All three needed to make changes if they were going to reconnect and stop living in a war zone. Both parents needed to learn how to mirror *and* set limits. They worked hard at it, although Dad had difficulty with the limit-setting while Mom struggled with the nurturing. And at first, Jillian simply couldn't or wouldn't see how her rude and condescending treatment of her parents was contributing to the problem.

Eventually I was able to get Jillian to understand that, like it or not, if she wanted more freedom and privileges, she needed to earn them by changing her behavior. If she wanted to go to the mall, for example, she needed to call home periodically as her parents had asked her to do. If she wanted to go to parties, she needed to honor the curfew they set instead of coming home late and then arguing about it. In short, if she wanted to be treated as an adult, she needed to start acting like one. Jillian didn't like it one bit: "That sucks! Why do I have to phone all the time? No one else has to do that." But she did finally agree to try it. And because they were all sincerely trying, her parents began to notice the change in her attitude and give her more privileges, while Jillian became more tolerant of the rules she couldn't get around. She stopped seeing rules as injuries, and began to make better decisions for herself.

I often explain to my teenage clients that if they want to be given the privileges that come with responsibility, they need to act like responsible teens, not little children. I advise them to come home a bit *before* their curfew for a while in order to show their parents that they're reliable and mature enough to be trusted.

However, it's important to remember that if your teen is in trouble, you first need to pull him back from the brink before you get to the part where he becomes responsible. To do that, everyone needs to be aware of the part they play in creating the family dynamic. If you and your spouse are at odds and angry with each other, it will be harder to work together. If everything the other one does annoys you, it will be much easier for your teen to pit you against each other. I call this the potato-chip phase of the relationship. If you're at the point with your spouse or partner where you're sitting on the couch watching TV while he (or she) is munching on a bag of chips, and the crunching is so irritating to you that you want to snatch the bag out of his hand, you know you're in a bad place. There's nothing wrong with having a disagreement or a difference of opinion, but when you're fighting constantly or you simply can't resolve your differences, it's time to get professional help. You may think that whatever issues you have with each other don't affect your teen, but they do. Teens hate it when their parents fight. It makes them both sad and angry, and that anger is manifested in their behavior. So again, the family dynamic affects everyone within the family unit: the teen's behavior affects the adults' relationship which affects the teen's behavior … and round and round it goes.

Children of Divorce

Sometimes when parents are divorced they're still able to work closely together to raise their children, and, of course, that's a best-case scenario. But often divorce leads to extreme polarization. And this provides the already manipulative teen with the ultimate opportunity to play one parent off against the other.

Most often the teen is closer to the custodial parent simply because that's the person with whom he spends the most time. But the custodial parent is also the one who does most of the disciplining, and is therefore the one most likely to bear the brunt of the teen's bad behavior. Because his time with the non-custodial parent is limited, he's more likely to avoid challenging that parent and to bring his anger or resentment home to the one with whom he feels safer and more comfortable. In addition, and for many of the same reasons, the non-custodial parent may take on the role of being a pal, the Disney Mom or Dad who wants to make the teen's visit all about breaking the rules and having fun.

If you're the custodial parent, and your son or daughter comes home from one of these freewheeling weekends with your former partner, don't get sucked into letting him bend or break the limits you've already established. He may be extra-sullen or silent for a day or two, but if you've built a firm foundation and the bond is strong, it can withstand the stress. In fact, your home is likely to become his oasis of calm, the place where he knows what to expect and what is expected of him, which—despite all the noise they make to the contrary—is what teens want. At the same time, however, if your teen is constantly complaining that you're too mean or too strict, it's a good idea to re-evaluate and make sure that the limits you're enforcing are reasonable. When our teens tell us the same thing over and over, there often is some truth to what they're saying.

Another thing to keep in mind is that even though a teenager may act as if he's completely comfortable with your divorce, he may still be sad, hurt, angry, or resentful about it. He might never admit it, but he may yearn for his parents to get back together. That yearning seems never to go away, even in the adult children of divorce. It doesn't mean you should remain in an unhappy or unhealthy marriage (which wouldn't be any better and could be much worse for your kids), but you should be aware of what they're almost certainly feeling even if they can't or won't express it. The best thing you can do to ease their sense of loss is make sure your own home is an oasis of safety, predictability, and love.

Not a Quick Fix but a Way of Life

If you've ever been on a diet you know that when you get a little complacent and don't stick with the program, the weight begins to creep back on. It's the same with mirroring and connecting. Your teen will continue to test you because that's part of the separation process, and so you'll need to keep it up. If you stop letting her know you're there holding onto the rope, she'll begin to feel disconnected and the unwanted behavior will come back. By the time our children become teenagers, the only control we really have over them is that connection. It's not what we give, promise, or threaten that gives us our authority; it's our relationship with them.

Too often, when the need to deal with a specific behavior has passed and the relationship begins to improve, parents quit employing the CALM technique. They fall back into more instinctive patterns and forget to do the incidental or conversational mirroring. Typically, when this happens both the parent's and the teen's behavior returns to the way it was. Your adolescent reverts to being rude or oppositional, and you revert to being angry and upset. I call it the elastic-band response. It's as if the emotional part of your brain is saying "No way! I'm not going back to that!" As a result, you find yourself overreacting and feeling defeated or depressed. Most if not all the families I work with go through this at some point. I tell them simply to start over, to go back to what they'd been doing before they stopped, and things will improve much more quickly than they did the first time.

This pattern of expansion and contraction will quite likely recur from time to time, and when it does you'll need to increase your mirroring, your consistent limit-setting, or both. Just keep in mind the analogy of the tension on the rope that needs constant adjustment and attention.

In the next chapter we'll be talking more about correcting and limit-setting, which is the other essential component of connected parenting.

FOUR

Letting Them Know
What You Expect

As you continue to CALM and reconnect, you'll find that your teen's behavior is changing. The kid who obstinately ignored your instructions to make her bed, put the dishes in the sink, or shut down the computer will, to your initial amazement, start to do those things without being asked. When that happens, how you react is as important as how you reacted when she was behaving badly. Let her know you noticed and that you appreciate it, but don't go overboard. If you're too effusive, not only will she be mortified (teens are easily mortified), but you'll be putting her under pressure to do it again. She'll worry that she can't and that you'll be disappointed in her, and rather than disappoint you she may well decide that it's better not to do it at all.

You need to notice the changes, but you also need to remember that your teen isn't perfect: he's going to make mistakes, act out, and want to do things you consider inappropriate or dangerous. Just remember that before you can correct or impose a consequence for unacceptable behavior, you need to mirror, or else your child will think you're being mean and he'll be unwilling or unable to hear what you're saying. Once the bond between you is strong enough, you'll be able to take on the hard tasks of correcting and coming up with consequences. It's vital that you get this right, because the stakes are higher for both of you now than they were when he was younger.

One of the most dramatic behavioral changes I've ever seen in a teen involved a boy named Sam who, by the time his parents came to me, had driven them to the absolute limit. Sam had been bullied at school; he hadn't attended in four months and was refusing to leave the house at all. As well as going into rages and making an enormous amount of emotional noise, he was going to bed at seven or eight o'clock in the morning, getting up at around four in the afternoon, and playing video games all night.

It's hard to imagine the pain everyone in this family was experiencing. Sam's parents were exhausted, frustrated, and heart-broken. Sam's older brother had been an easygoing and successful teen. Now they were not only worried about Sam's ability to function in the world, but also humiliated by his behavior and what they perceived to be their failure. They'd tried begging, arguing, threatening—basically everything they could think of—and were now at a total loss.

As matters stood, the bond between Sam and his parents had become so frayed that he'd perceive any consequences they imposed as injuries. They needed to concentrate on soft parenting first in order to repair that bond. This was no one's fault: it was the dynamic created by years of his behavior and their quite naturally pulling away to protect themselves. Becoming aware of how those defenses had exacerbated the problem had to be their first step toward change.

They were skeptical at first, but they were desperate and willing to try anything. They put their hearts into applying the CALM technique, and after just a couple of months, Sam's mood began to improve. Now I suggested that it was time for them to introduce some hard parenting. They started by trying to get him to go to bed by three a.m., telling him that if he didn't, the computer would be gone in the morning. Sam cursed them out and ranted and raved and didn't keep the curfew. So, when he finally did fall asleep, they took all the keyboards from all the computers in the house.

I had instructed them not to grab them from him in anger, not to act on impulse or when everyone in the family was in fight-or-flight mode. This is extremely important. One of the biggest mistakes parents make is to grab the cellphone or laptop out of their teen's hands once a consequence has been established and understood. That's a recipe for disaster, and will result in two people who are both in fight-or-flight mode engaging in a wrestling match. The only effective way to do it is to calmly tell your teen that if he doesn't hand over the item it will only be gone longer. Then wait until he's asleep to take the device or call your cellphone company, inform them that you've lost the phone, and ask them to suspend service.

When Sam got up he ransacked the house, ripped the door off the cupboard where the keyboards were locked away, and played video games all day. Still, his parents remained calm. When the same thing happened the following night, they removed the keyboards from the house. That's when he stole the car keys from his mother's purse. He didn't drive the car; he just took the keys to demonstrate that he too could play their game. But again, his parents didn't react; they simply took cabs where they needed to go. In other words, each time Sam upped the ante they found a way around him, and of course, they continued to mirror and explain what would happen if he didn't comply. When he saw that his actions weren't having the desired effect, he returned the keys.

After about a month of this routine, Sam's parents noticed that he was cleaning up after himself, putting his dishes away, even emptying the dishwasher when they asked him to. And he was going to bed by one o'clock and getting up by nine or ten in the morning.

I began working with Sam one-on-one and using cognitive behavioral therapy to address his anxiety. He'd been taking anti-anxiety medication for quite some time, but he also needed a safe, neutral place where he could talk about his issues and develop strategies for dealing with them. We then began to work on a plan for getting him to begin participating in life. At first he agreed to go to the gym and work out a couple of times a week. Then, after a while, he agreed to take a high school course online. Finally, he began attending an alternative school and got a part-time job at a fast-food restaurant.

Sam, who'd been on the brink of being completely lost, has now completed his first year at university where he's studying integrative cyber arts. I recently received an email from him telling me about how great his first year had been, how many friends he'd made, and how much he loved all his courses. He has turned into a delightful, responsible young man who enjoys a close relationship with his parents.

Sam's case may be special, but only in degree; the routines and techniques that helped him are basically the same ones I recommend to all parents. One of the keys to his parents' success was their ability (difficult as it was) to maintain their equilibrium: it is absolutely essential to remain calm and neutral as you correct and impose consequences. If you fly into a rage or burst into tears, you'll be sending the message that, on the one hand, your teenager has succeeded in getting to you, and on the other hand, that you're not strong enough to keep him safe—which is what he really wants and needs.

The more you and your teen have become disconnected, the more likely you are to respond emotionally. You may be thinking, *Why is my kid so ungrateful?* or *What a spoiled brat!* when what you should be thinking is *Something is wrong here. What can I do to help him and make it right?* Bad behavior is your teen's way of communicating that he has a problem, and your job as a parent is to help him find a solution. But too often, instead we get mad: *Well, if that's the way he's going to be just wait until the next time he wants me to do something for him.* Then you sit back and wait for him to apologize, which probably isn't going to happen (or if it does, it's for the wrong reasons). It's a standoff, with both of you metaphorically standing there with your arms crossed. Meanwhile you haven't taught your child anything, and because adolescents and teens are so sensitive to attachment issues, you may have actually widened the breach between you. When that happens, everyone loses and everyone gets hurt.

Letting Them Know It's Their Choice

By the time a child reaches the age of fourteen or fifteen he needs to feel that he has some control over his own destiny. If you let him know that a behavior is unacceptable and he continues that behavior, he has, in effect, made a choice. And if you also let him know in advance what the consequence of continuing that behavior will be, he's chosen that too. I call this process frontloading.

When you're deciding on a consequence, you need to think about what would be appropriate. If the consequence is too severe you probably won't stick to it (which can be even worse than not having imposed a consequence at all), and if it's too mild your kid will just shrug it off. It's important to establish consequences that fit the crime, so to speak. In fact, you can actually work with your teen to come up with these limits together.

Let's say you know your teenage daughter is texting her friends well into the wee hours of the morning. You would frontload by saying, "You know, if you're up texting your friends until two in the morning you're not getting enough sleep, and I wouldn't be a good parent if I continued allowing that to happen because you really need your sleep. So here's the deal. You've got the next four nights to show me you can handle this yourself, and if you can't, you're telling me with your words that you can but you're showing me with your behavior that you can't. So I'm going to have to help you. I'm going to take the phone at ten o'clock every night until we can figure out how you can handle this better, and then we'll try it again." She'll undoubtedly yell, "I hate you. You're the worst parent in the world!" So you say, "You know, honey, this is a choice you made. You had an opportunity to handle it yourself and chose not to, so you should really be mad at yourself." Stay calm and neutral, expect the emotional noise we've talked about, and hold your ground.

Incidentally, sleep is a real problem for teens. If you think it's important for your teen to get enough sleep, you're right. Although optimal sleep for teens is nine hours a night, a survey conducted by the Centers for Disease Control found that, of the more than 12,000 high school students surveyed, only 900 reported getting the optimal amount. More than 30 percent (about 3600 students) reported getting seven hours, 2700 (22.8 percent) got six hours, 1200 (10 percent) got five hours, and 708 or 5.9 percent got four hours or less.

These numbers are disturbing for several reasons. Lack of sleep has been linked to poor performance in school, headaches, depression, mood swings, and dangerous driving. In addition, it's been shown that the amygdala—the part of the brain that processes anxiety—is 60 percent more reactive when we don't get enough sleep. Because we're tired we're less aware of what's going on around us, and thus more likely to be caught in a dangerous situation. To our primitive brain, that means we're more likely to be eaten by a lion or tiger because we didn't see it coming. So our brain tries to keep us alive by making us more agitated and jumpy (or reactive) and more likely to notice when something is bothering us.

You might want to explain all this to your daughter when you're talking about why she needs to get more sleep. Mirror first, and then frontload by helping her understand the consequences of not getting enough sleep, not only in terms of the limits you decided upon but also in terms of what's happening in her brain. Some kids will listen to your explanation; some will just tell you they don't believe it; and some will think about it and perhaps try to change their behavior on their own.

You can also use the frontloading technique when you know you're about to walk into a situation that could be problematic. Let's say the family is going out to dinner on Friday with your friends and their son, Mike. Mike is about the same age as your son, Charlie, but Charlie thinks Mike is a dork. You know this, so before the event, you have a little frontloading conversation with your son. "Charlie, you know we're going out to dinner with the Joneses on Friday and they're going to be bringing Mike. I know Mike isn't your favorite person, and you don't need to be his friend, but for this one evening I know you can be polite and respectful to him, so I'd really appreciate if you could do that. I don't think that's asking too much, and if you can't make the effort then I'm afraid you'll be staying home on Saturday and miss hanging out with your friends."

When you mirror and frontload, there's less chance you'll wind up yelling at your son later, after he's spent Friday evening sitting like a sullen lump and refusing to talk to Mike at all. And if that's what he's done, you can state calmly that he's made his choice and will be spending his Saturday at home. When you yell at a little kid, he might cry or have a tantrum, but you can send him to his room or just let him scream it out. The problem with having a screaming match with a teenager is that he or she is likely to storm out of the house and disappear into the night, which is exactly what happened to the parents of one of my clients.

Cynthia is a dramatic, challenging kid who tends to use behavior as a way to express her feelings. One day she discovered that her younger sister had used one of her hair products, and she began to chase her around the room. Had she actually been hitting her sister Cynthia's mother would have had to deal with that immediately, but in this case, even though Cynthia was clearly in full fight-or-flight mode, there was no physical violence occurring. Cynthia's mother—who before this incident had been doing very well with her mirroring—just snapped and screamed, "That does it, you're totally grounded. No phone, no TV, no nothing. Your behavior is disgusting!" It might have been more helpful for her to use the CALM technique and say something like "Okay, obviously something really huge has happened here. Cynthia, you don't usually do this, so please help me understand what's happening. What do I need to know?" She would have had to express herself with the right amount of urgency—not panic, just a serious "let's get to the bottom of this" kind of tone to get Cynthia's attention. And then, after a making a few CALMing statements, she could have addressed the behavior and discussed possible consequences. But she didn't do that, and what happened next is that Cynthia stormed out the back door and disappeared. It was ten-thirty at night, and her parents wound up driving all over the neighborhood in the dark searching for her. Luckily they found her sitting in a nearby park under a tree, but it could have been much worse.

Many parents are so afraid their teens will do what Cynthia did that they don't impose consequences at all. It's terrifying to think your teen could simply walk out altogether, which is exactly why, for many teens, threatening to take off is a kind of trump card. If your teen is rebellious and frequently pushes boundaries, those threats can be even more frightening. But if she's firmly attached to you, that isn't going to happen because she perceives home as a place of safety. Adolescents need to think of their home as a safe place, not somewhere they need to escape from—which is, again, why it's always so important to secure the attachment first. If instead you begin with containment, the teen is just going to rebel.

Of course, you won't always be in a situation where you can frontload. Kids are really great at coming up with surprises. When this happens and you're caught off guard, you need to get hold of yourself and avoid acting spontaneously out of anger. Acting in the heat of the moment usually results in imposing too heavy a consequence. Your burst of anger is meant to get him upset, but teens rarely give you that kind of satisfaction. Instead they're likely to shrug and say something like "See if I care," which in turn leads to your saying, "Oh, yeah, well then what about this ..." and upping the ante even further. By the time you're done, the kid has no incentive to improve his behavior because you've already taken away everything there was to take. If you find yourself yelling and it feels fantastic, you're in fight-or-flight mode. You need to stop and think: *Is this something I want to say, or is it something my teen needs to hear?* It's a question of using your frontal lobe.

Step back, take a deep breath, and say, "You know, there's going to be some kind of consequence for this. I'm going to take a moment to think about what it should be because right now I'm so mad that I'm likely to give you one that's too severe. And you too need to think about what a reasonable consequence will be." In this way you avoid the mistakes that can come with reacting impulsively, and you also model the virtues of thinking before you act. And when you ask your teen to participate and come up with a consequence for himself, you'll often be surprised to find that he comes up with something more severe than anything you would have thought of. Finally, if you do just lose it—as we all do from time to time—you can always go back and say, "You know, I did that because I was angry," and then revise the consequence you gave—with the understanding that if your teen doesn't handle it well the original one will be reinstated.

Most parents get especially upset when their kids swear or curse at them. Of course that behavior is unacceptable, but you need to remember what we've discussed concerning impulse control and brain development. Because they can't always use their frontal lobe to mediate behavior, and because they're experiencing such wild hormone shifts, teens sometimes use their parents as a way to regulate themselves. Kids have told me that they can actually feel the pent-up energy surging through their bodies. So they let it all out on you, get a big rush of adrenaline, and then they feel better. You've probably done much the same thing when you just needed to blow off steam. You can still let your child know that you don't want to be spoken to that way—just don't do it when you're in the middle of a fight (which is probably what caused him to curse in the first place). If you find yourself on the verge of reacting to a barrage of swear words, try to stay neutral and simply say, "You know what? I'm not going to take this. I like myself too much. I'm going to walk away."

It's also critical that you speak to your teen in the same way you'd like him to speak to you. If you pay attention, you might be surprised to discover how many times in any given day adults speak disrespectfully to teenagers.

Staying neutral is hard, but it's important. And it may help you to remember that their behavior is related to normal brain development. Kids really do carry around a lot of stress, and because their frontal lobe isn't fully developed, they can't always use that part of their brain to regulate their emotions. So, in effect, they borrow yours. They may have had a tough day at school, a fight with a friend, or some other stressful encounter, so when they come home and you innocently ask them to hang up their coat, they release all that pent-up emotion by going off on you.

Daniel Amen puts it this way: "Many people with prefrontal cortex [frontal lobe] problems tend to be conflict-seeking to stimulate their brain." It stands to reason, then, that a teen with an undeveloped prefrontal cortex would pick a fight with you just for the nice jolt of adrenaline, which helps bring the brain back into balance so that he feels fine again. But, as Amen notes, "It's critical for you not to feed the turmoil but rather to starve it. The more someone with the pattern annoyingly tries to upset or injure you, the more you need to be quiet, calm, and steady." The reason is this: "In general conflict-seeking people are used to being able to get you upset. They've mastered all your emotional buttons and they push them regularly. [So true of teens!] When you begin to deny the drama and the adrenaline rush [by remaining neutral] they initially react negatively, but then they become able to calm." So, if you deny your teen the opportunity to regulate off you, he'll gradually become better able to self-regulate. If, on the other hand, you get sucked in, he'll get into the habit of seeking you out every time he needs to let off some steam. You inadvertently become part of his coping mechanism.

If you're in a rough place with your teen and have been at odds for a while, you may have to get creative about how to stay calm and not get angry. When you're ready to explode, try to remember that, strange as it seems, you're really going to miss that kid when he's gone. Try uploading a batch of baby pictures onto your computer and putting them in slide-show mode as a way of reminding yourself that this kid is still your baby. If you walk away from the battle you can go back later, when you've both calmed down. Do some mirroring about how frustrated he must have been, and then say, "I know swearing feels good. It's such a relief to just get it out. I totally get it. But it's not acceptable to me and I won't be spoken to that way. So you've got a few days to show me that you're really working on this. Maybe think of other words you could use when you feel like swearing at me. But if you can't do it, if after [whatever timeframe you decide on] you're still doing it, you're showing that you can't do it on your own and I need to do something about it. What that means is every time you swear, your phone [or the computer or whatever you choose] will be gone for [whatever period of time seems appropriate to you]." And, as always, be prepared to follow through with the consequence.

It's Okay to Negotiate

As long as you've mirrored so that your teen knows you've heard her and understand where she's coming from, it's possible for you to negotiate. You might consider doing that when she asks for something you're reluctant to agree to, such as a party or a trip without adult supervision.

Let's say your seventeen-year-old daughter wants to go with her friends to a classmate's summer house for the weekend when her parents will be away. First of all, remember that this is *huge* for her, the equivalent of your being invited to spend the weekend on Grand Cayman Island with all the senior vice-presidents of your company. How would you feel if your spouse or partner said, "Well, honey, I don't think that's a very good idea"? I'm not suggesting that you agree to let your daughter go, just that you show her you understand what saying no will mean to her. Here's how that conversation would typically play out.

DAUGHTER: Mom, some of the kids in my class are going to Jennie's parents' summer house this weekend. Can I go?

YOU: Are Jennie's parents going to be there?

DAUGHTER: Well, no, but her older brother is going.

At that point your inclination is probably to just say no. But if you do that without mirroring first, your daughter is going to feel that you didn't understand the urgency of her request, so she'll keep sending the message: "But Mom, everyone is going! All the other kids' parents are letting them [which could very well be true]. You're just being mean."

By now you'll probably be so annoyed with her whining that you start to react to the behavior instead of the request, and the original focus of the conversation will be lost. The discussion escalates into slamming doors and I-hate-yous that could go on for days.

So here's a better way to go about it.

First, you park your own agenda for the moment and let your daughter know that you're listening to her and that you want to understand the importance of what she's asking. You can say, "Okay, my instinct is to freak out about this, but tell me what I need to know about the trip, why it's so important, and why you think you should be able to go."

Your teen will start talking, and now you need to make a couple of open-ended mirroring statements, such as "So, *everyone* in your whole group is going and you believe everyone else's parents are okay with that. No wonder you think it would be mean of me to say no."

Your daughter will sense that you're not happy with the situation but that you're at least willing to listen—and that's all true: you're not being disingenuous in any way.

After a few of those mirroring statements and after she's gotten it all out, you can say, "You know, I understand why you want to go. I can see why you think this is really important and that if you don't go you'll be missing out on a great opportunity. But here's the problem: I'm really not comfortable with it, I don't think it's safe, and I don't think it's appropriate for a group of kids your age to go away without an adult. I know your friends are telling you that their parents think it's okay, but I don't think it's okay, and I love you enough to say no." At this point you can use the CALM technique to empathize with how hard it is for her not to be able to go. You can step into her shoes, show that you understand the situation, and still hold firm to your belief that it's not okay to go.

Depending on the situation and how you feel about it, you can also try to work out some kind of compromise: she can go but she has to sleep at a nearby relative's house, or she can go but you're going to pick her up at a predetermined time. But if you can't come to such an agreement, you need to stick to the limit you've set.

Your decision is likely to lead to a lot of emotional noise, but you need to be brave enough to say, "I respect that you're freaking out about this. I get it. I understand why you're mad, but calling me names and saying hurtful things isn't going to help, and if you keep it up the whole thing is off the table and you will not be going at all. I like myself too much to be treated like this and I love you enough for you to be angry with me." Then you just walk away and let her have her tantrum. If your connection is strong enough she'll huff and puff and then she'll stop and get over it.

Kids need you to set these boundaries, and they have to push back—that's their job. Your job is to keep the right tension on the rope so that they feel your presence, and to be consistent in the boundaries you set so that they know what to expect. Many parents report that their kids get over these confrontations very quickly. In fact, they're sometimes relieved to be able to use you as an excuse for not doing something that scares them a little but that they think they must do to keep up with their peers. It's much easier to say "My parents are being stupid and won't let me go" than it is to admit something is scary and they aren't comfortable with it.

Your teen may sulk over the weekend, knowing that "all the other kids" are at this great house party, but you can mirror that, too. Don't try to be sugary sweet or suggest that she go to the movies with you. That's annoying and would just set her off all over again. Respect the fact that she's upset and try to think about how you would have felt at her age. Give her respect and some space. Remember to use the CALM technique in a subtle, conversational way to speed up the repair process. And when she does come out of her room and act like a human being, please resist the urge to ooh and aah about how your little girl is back. Don't hold a parade! Just be normal—and appreciate how nice normal can be.

That Big Galoot Is Still Your Child

It can be intimidating to have to reprimand or discipline a teenage boy who's a foot and a half taller than you and bellowing in his newly acquired deep voice. Kids—particularly boys—seem to go from cute and cuddly to big and scary in the blink of an eye. And many clients have told me that they *can't* discipline their teen because he or she will just ignore them. That simply isn't true. Despite everything they may say or do to the contrary, your kids actually *want* you to say what you mean and mean what you say. It's when they sense you're uncertain that they become anxious, and that's when they're most likely to act out.

FIVE

What Parents Fear Most

Many if not most teens will experiment at some time with sex, drugs, and alcohol, but for the vast majority it doesn't go beyond experimenting. They'll try it, learn from the experience, and survive just fine. Still, these are the three biggies for us as parents because we know how dangerous they can be.

The problem is that most kids live so entirely in the moment that they simply don't think about the consequences their actions might have in what they see as the far distant—and therefore irrelevant—future. Yet adolescents today are expected to make decisions about issues many of them are not mature enough to make without the help and guidance of an adult. And the closer your relationship to your teen, the more she'll seek, trust, and value your input.

Sex and Teens

Kids are being sexualized earlier and earlier—particularly girls. Some parents may think it's cute to buy little girls mini-grownup clothes (including tiny push-up bras) or to watch them "dance" to a music video, but what they're learning from that—particularly when they receive positive feedback from adults—comes back to bite us when those same little girls become tweens and then teens.

The sexualization of teens is all over the media—you can't miss it. If you haven't seen the movies teens watch these days, you might want to rent one: it may give you some insight into their world.

For an enormous number of teens, sex has become so trivialized that it's just another routine activity, not much different from going to the mall. And for many, oral sex (with a nod of thanks to former president Clinton) isn't considered sex at all. Hook-up parties are nothing more than the latest version of the key party, that seventies phenomenon in which couples got together and threw their house keys in a bowl, with the key they drew determining their sexual partner for the evening. The only difference is that kids have streamlined the process by doing away with the keys. And as a woman and the mother of two daughters, I'm concerned about the pressure on girls today to "serve" or "pleasure" boys.

I often lead girls' empowerment groups, and young girls talk to me about the images they see on TV of male pop stars and rappers fully clothed while the female stars are scantily dressed and hanging on to a stripper's pole. They also talk about hook-ups (getting together for sex without commitment) and grinding (a way of dancing where a boy comes up behind a girl, grinds into her, and then moves on to another partner). Many girls have mixed feelings about these encounters: excited and intrigued on the one hand, frightened and uncomfortable on the other. Many also feel that they have to go along with the group in order to be popular.

We know that girls today are reaching puberty earlier than previous generations did, but that doesn't mean their brains or emotions have kept up with their bodies. I certainly want girls to have a healthy sense of themselves and their sexuality, but I don't believe this self-awareness comes from their ability to please the opposite sex. By making themselves so easily available, they also send a dangerous and confusing message to boys. If the guys grow up believing that it's their right to expect sexual favors from girls, what happens when a girl refuses? How should they react? Are the boys who feel entitled to easy sex the same ones who, in a few years, might be involved in date rape? Too much sexual activity at too early an age also puts pressure on the boys, who may not be ready but who can't very well refuse without running the risk of being teased or ridiculed by their peers. Both girls and boys need to learn, when they're ready to handle it, how to have balanced, healthy, and reciprocal sexual relationships.

Talking to Teens About Sex

What you don't want to do is have "the sex conversation" with your teen—unless, of course, you just want to give him a good laugh, because most of them are way ahead of you in that department. Most teens find out about sex from their friends and TV. Nevertheless, there are times when you do talk to your teen about sex, either because he or she has asked you a question or because you think it's important to have a conversation about the potential consequences of some sexually charged activity, such as sexting (sending sexual text messages or photos on a cellphone) or sexual abuse (either mental or physical).

I can't give you a script for those conversations, because how you choose to approach the subject will be very personal and will depend both on your own comfort level and that of your child. I can, however, give you a few guidelines.

If your teen asks you a question about your personal life, past or present, and you don't feel comfortable answering it, it's perfectly okay to say that. The good news is that these questions are unlikely to be asked: most of the kids I talk to are horrified at the thought of their parents having sex. They don't want to even think about it, let alone talk about it. But if your teen proves to be the exception, instead of answering directly you could give examples of other kids you knew, which would deflect attention from you. Or you could say something like "You know, I have to tell you, I'm really uncomfortable with this. It's very personal and I'll need some time to think about it. If I give you information you're not ready to hear, that wouldn't be a good idea, and if I don't give you enough information you might just make your own decision without any guidance from me. I want to do a good job with this, so I want to think about it." Kids are usually okay with that. What's important is that they know you're taking them seriously.

Parents sometimes ask me what they should do when their teen comes back and says, "So, have you thought about it?" or if she never comes back at all. Well, if she doesn't come back, she's forgotten about it and probably doesn't really want to know. If she does, she really wants an answer, which is why you should take the time to think about it in the first place. How you answer will depend on your own comfort level as well as the age and maturity of your child. If you recall the books on child development you may have read, they generally provide some kind of timeline for when your baby will start to do one thing or another—roll over, sit up, walk, say his first words, and so on. You might also recall that if your child didn't do what he was supposed to do at exactly the right time, you got a little (or a lot) upset. Well, just as there's no precise moment when a toddler should start to walk, there's no absolute rule for what you should or shouldn't discuss with your teenager at any specific age. You know your own child, and you know what he or she is capable of understanding. There's nothing wrong with telling a younger or less mature adolescent that you believe the question is important and you'll feel more comfortable discussing it when he or she is a bit older. The answer may make him mad, but he'll walk away. Whatever you do, don't lie. If you lie your kids will sense it, and you'll lose your credibility right there. Or else the lie will come back to haunt you when the truth inadvertently pops out of your mouth somewhere down the road and the kid says, "But I thought you told me ..."

If, on the other hand, you think *you* need to initiate a conversation, whether it's about sex or any other serious subject, timing may be everything. Consider what else is going on in the family or in your child's life. What kind of mood is she in? What kind of mood are you in?

I've found that talking to your teen (particularly to a boy) while you're in the car (assuming you're alone) works well because you're both looking ahead rather than directly at each other, and that can help you both feel more comfortable. That said, you don't want to make a habit of having difficult conversations every time you get in the car. If you do that, your teen will begin to dread getting in the car with you. You also don't want to push so hard that he shuts down and begins to feel like a prisoner in the passenger seat. If your kid loves to talk in the car and that's when you're most likely to find out what's going on in his life, that's great. But don't expect it to happen every time. And if one day he's chatting away and the next day he's silent, resist the urge to say, "What's the matter with you? Didn't we have a great conversation yesterday? Why won't you talk to me?" Instead you could say something like "You know, I'd love to talk to you, but I can tell you're not into it today, and that's okay. It makes me a little sad, but it's okay." Then back off and put some music on. He may start to talk spontaneously, or maybe he won't, but he'll be more likely to talk tomorrow or the next day.

If not in the car, then try talking to your teen at night before bed, when you're both relaxed, or in the context of something else, such as a television movie or an item on a news broadcast. Whatever you do, keep the tone neutral. If you see an item about a teen caught up in a sexting scandal, for example, resist the urge to shriek, "DO YOU DO THAT? DO YOUR FRIENDS DO THAT?" Bite your tongue and come back to it later, when you're not so freaked out and can present the problem clearly and calmly.

In the end, you need to realize that no single conversation is going to make a huge difference to your relationship. It's the overall effect of many, many mirroring conversations about things that have nothing to do with sex. The more of those mirroring moments you have, the more loved and valued your child will feel. And when a child feels that way she'll be much more likely to value herself, to be more resilient and self-reliant, and to make better decisions— despite what her peers may be doing. Your challenge as a parent is to hold on to that thought through all the "I hate you. You're ruining my life and you're embarrassing me" episodes you're bound to experience with your teen.

Alcohol and Teens

At the risk of sounding as if I think it's okay for kids to drink alcohol (which I don't), it's almost inevitable that, at some point, most kids will experiment. When teens are drinking, there aren't any adults around to help them process the implications of what they're doing. So they need to be bonded enough to you to carry your voice in their head when you're not there.

A surprising number of parents today seem to think that because their teens will inevitably drink alcohol, the best way to keep them safe is to buy it for them so that they're drinking with their friends at home. Is this a good choice? It's a complicated problem. In some parts of the world, drinking, especially wine with dinner, is not considered inappropriate for teens. In most of North America, of course, this is illegal, and we must consider the implications of inadvertently allowing teens to believe that it's okay sometimes to disobey the law. Another factor to consider is the effect on your teenager's friends. Do they bring a note from their parents saying it's okay for them to drink at your house? What are they going to do when they leave your house? What is your legal, moral, and ethical responsibility for *their* well-being? Depending on where you live, you may have some legal responsibility as an adult who "knowingly or recklessly" serves alcohol to minors. So if a teen drinks in your home and subsequently harms either himself or someone else, you may suffer legal consequences. That in itself ought to be reason enough not to do it. (And just because "everyone else's" parents do it definitely doesn't mean that you should.) And finally, you need to consider whether your teen is going to differen-tiate between when it's okay to drink and when it isn't, or to know when he's had enough and stop. If you know your child well and he or she seems able to make reasonably good choices, you may relax a bit and trust him to work through it. But many kids aren't very good at self-monitoring in the best of circumstances, and when they've had a couple of drinks what little ability they might normally possess is certainly no longer working.

I've heard too many stories about parties where alcohol was served and kids trashed their host's house. Maybe you think your teen would never let that happen, or that his or her friends would never do that. And maybe you're right. But I'm sure that's exactly what the parents whose houses were vandalized thought too. The problem is that your teen invites his friends, who then invite their friends, who then tell other kids, and before you know it total strangers are showing up at your door. Social networking sites like Facebook also play a role here, because kids are likely to post what they're doing or where they're going without giving a thought to the potential viral spread of that information. When strangers or uninvited party crashers do show up at the door, it's the rare teen who, even if he wants to, will be strong enough mentally, and perhaps even physically, to refuse them entrance. And the further removed the crasher is from the person whose home he's in, the less he cares about that person's property.

One dad I know did absolutely everything right when his seventeen-year-old son had a Halloween party. Both parents were at home and the dad made periodic appearances to "refill the chip bowl" or for some other reason. The party started out relatively small, but more and more kids began to arrive and at one point the son refused entrance to a group of kids who came to the door. They pushed their way in anyway, and when Dad came down the stairs his son was in the midst of a full-blown fist fight with one of them. Then the crashers attacked the father, and the son was hit over the head with a bottle. Finally someone called 911. The police arrived and the crashers ran out the back door, but the bottle-wielder was found and arrested. It was, to say the least, a traumatic situation, not only for the host but also for the teens who were legitimate guests.

Teens can be extremely dramatic and persistent. They know how to wear us down with their stomping and wailing and moaning that "everyone else's parents buy them alcohol" (which, unfortunately, may be true) and the "You're ruining my life!" accusatory refrain. And if you've been giving in to their tantrums ever since they were four years old and simply *had to have* that toy they saw advertised on television, it's going to be particularly hard to refuse them now. But the beauty of this parenting model is that it's never too late to turn things around. There's almost nothing you may have done in the past—if it was done with love and the best of intentions—that will prevent you from doing something different now and in the future. I tell my clients all the time to say to their children, "I love you enough for you to hate me for this." Be prepared to say those words to your teen a million times in a thousand different ways. And, I hasten to point out, it's not the same as saying "I'm doing this for your own good." If you've been mirroring—and you *always must* mirror *before* you make a containing statement—she'll probably stomp around and slam a couple of doors and make a lot of noise, but she'll live and she'll get through it.

So if you don't buy the alcohol, won't your teenager figure out how to get it some other way? Yes, almost certainly. If you say no will she get mad, storm out of the house, and never come back? In my experience, that is rare. She may storm out of the house, but—except in extremely rare cases—she will come back. And again, the more connected she is to you, the better able she'll be to feel the tension on the rope, the less vulnerable she'll be to peer pressure, and the worse she'll feel about disappointing you.

Any child, whether he's a toddler or a teen, wants to know that you're not afraid and that you're the captain of the plane steering a steady course through turbulence, away from danger, and in the right direction. They don't want to hang out with the captain and eat dinner with him every night, but they do want him to be confident and in control. So if you're sending mixed signals or allowing them to intimidate you, ultimately they'll be more, not less anxious. I see this dynamic play out all the time. Teens will do everything in their power to intimidate Mom, and then if she breaks down and cries or looks weak, they'll hate her for her weakness and themselves for having caused her to cry. If you already have a strong relationship with your teen and you cry it can be okay; but if you have a difficult relationship, crying often makes the problem worse. Whatever the conversation is about—sex, alcohol, drugs, or anything else—you need to sound confident and authoritative.

Teens want you to be strong. They don't want to be able to intimidate you. If you cry and get upset they'll see this as weakness, especially if you do it a lot. And if you yell and scream they'll see it as weakness as well—a sign that they've been able to get to you. Particularly if they haven't gotten their own way about something, they'll keep at you and get really nasty in an effort to take you down with them or to punish you so that you'll think twice about holding your ground the next time. Again, it's vitally important to use the CALM technique, and then to stay neutral and stay firm. If you lose your temper and say all kinds of hurtful or nasty things, they'll only feel more justified in the behavior that triggered your reaction in the first place. Using empathy is the only way to get them to reflect on their own behavior.

What If Your Teen Does Come Home Drunk?

If he does come home from a party drunk out of his mind and sick as a dog (assuming it's the first time and not habitual), your handling of the situation may determine whether or not his drinking becomes a pattern with a significant impact on his life. You definitely don't want to get involved in a big fight about it while he's still drunk. That would only create more stress on the bond and could easily wind up with your teen doing it again just to get back at you. What you want to do instead is start mirroring: "It's so horrible to feel this way. It's such an awful feeling to be this sick and it's so hard with alcohol to know what your body will do." In this way you're fully empathizing with his situation and helping him get through it. Save your own agenda for the morning. Choose a time when your teen is feeling well enough to listen but not so well that he's already forgotten how sick he felt. If he's already feeling embarrassed, guilty, or ashamed, he might be more willing to talk to you about it.

Unless he's so sick that you honestly think it's a medical emergency, try not to be too helpful. If you make it too easy by standing by with a cold cloth and a glass of water, he may not remember quite how awful it was. So, after you've mirrored, step back and let him feel what he's feeling—which is, in fact, a natural consequence of his actions.

You want him to know that you're taking this seriously but also to give him enough rope to figure out what he's going to do the next time. The point of the rope analogy here is that you can't do the climbing for him, but you can let him know you're still there. Teens climb higher and choose steeper cliffs than younger kids, which makes it scarier for parents. And some kids need to be kept on a shorter rope than others. Drinking alcohol is about self-regulation, and teens who have problems with that in other areas will have more problems with alcohol as well.

If he does come home in a similarly drunk condition again, use the CALM technique. You might say, "I gave you the chance to prove you could handle this and it was too much for you, so I'm going to have to say no more parties until you can show me that you're mature enough to make better choices." Just try not to add, "I knew this would happen! I knew I shouldn't have let you talk me into it!" The point always is to help your teen understand that privileges are earned.

Drugs and Teens

While drugs are comparable to alcohol in many ways, there are significant differences between them. In the hands of adolescents, drugs can be both more dangerous and more insidious than alcohol. Many kids are taking prescription drugs for attention deficit hyper-activity disorder (ADHD) or some other diagnosed condition, so they've been taught that at least some drugs are good for them. But not all kids like the way their meds make them feel. They know their prescription drugs have street value, and some may be trading the drug they're supposed to take for others they'd rather take. And drugs are often easier to obtain than alcohol. Your teen may need an older person to buy alcohol for his party, but he can get all kinds of drugs on his own, probably more easily than you can. And anyone who sells street drugs to a child is clearly not concerned with the child's well-being.

Many parents find it difficult to talk to their kids about drugs, especially if they experimented themselves when they were younger. They're afraid of the big question: "Didn't you do the same thing when you were my age?" How do you answer that? It's like answering questions about sex: there isn't a right or wrong response. It depends on your personal ethics, your comfort level, and the relationship you have with your child. You might be comfortable saying "No, I didn't" (if that's true) or "Yes, I did. And these are the mistakes I made. If I had it to do over, I wish ..." and then going into whatever regrets you might have for the choices you made. Or you might say, "I'm not comfortable answering that question. When you're older, I'll answer it." Or, "You know, I'd like to take some time to think about this conversation so that I handle it the best way I can." And again, I don't recommend lying: chances are the truth will come out eventually, and then you'll have trust issues to deal with.

It's a good idea to let your teen know you're aware that many kids do use drugs. You could say, for example, "I know that kids your age experiment, especially when you're in a group and it's more difficult for you to make an individual choice. But you need to be aware of your own comfort level and know that you're not going to be more popular just because you go along with something other people are doing." Try to get your teen to recognize the feeling she gets when she makes a good or bad decision. When you make a decision you know is right, you feel stronger. You actually feel a surge of strength. When you make a doubtful decision you feel a little bit sick, a little bit weaker. Remind her of a time when she made a good or bad decision and the physical feelings that went along with it. You might even recount an occasion when you had those feelings yourself. You can also explain that while embarking on illegal, illicit, or dangerous behavior gives you an adrenaline rush, the brain soon gets used to the sensation and then you have to keep upping the ante to get the same rush.

The more open and honest you can be with your teen, the better the conversation will go. And the closer your relationship, the less likely he'll be tempted to blindly follow his peers or to self-medicate to reduce feelings of anxiety. He might still experiment, but he may also be more likely to think, *That didn't feel so good. I don't want to feel that way again.* Many teens are able to make good decisions, and often we don't give them enough credit for that. But if they're feeling disconnected, there's a subconscious aspect to their decision-making. By choosing to do drugs, they may be sending the message *My life sucks. I'm going to push this over the edge so that my parents will finally realize how miserable I am.*

And some kids don't always have a lot of common sense, or an awareness of their own mortality. They do stupid stuff, and when they're stoned, doing stupid stuff is a lot easier. In the end, we try to equip our children with the instinctive wisdom and the gumption to say no to self-destructive behavior—or at least to stop before they get to the things that are really dangerous. While many (if not most) kids experiment with drugs, very few of them develop a drug problem or become addicted. Some kids, however, are just plain risk-takers, and they're the ones most likely to be looking for the next best high, which is never too hard to come by. Whether it's sniffing Dust-Off computer-screen cleaner or smoking *salvia divinorum*—a legal, mind-altering herb said to produce a quick, intense, short-lived hallucinogenic state—there will always be kids reckless enough to try.

Just remember (the core idea I always return to) that if your teen feels connected to you, and if his brain is exposed to the natural reward chemicals like oxytocin that come from feeling loved and being bonded, the circuitry for attachment will increase and he won't crave the dangerous, short-lived chemical high that comes from taking drugs.

If You Think Your Teen Has a Drug Problem

Many of the so-called warning signs that your teen has a drug problem can also be manifestations of normal teen behaviors. Keeping that in mind, here are some of the signs we're told to look for:

- Chronic eye redness
- Runny nose
- Dilated or constricted pupils
- Radical mood shifts
- Changes in eating or sleeping patterns
- Money missing from parents' wallets

If you do suspect that your teen is using drugs, the key test is to compare the way he is now to the way he was before your worries were triggered. If he's had a runny nose for as long as you can remember, it may not mean anything now. If, however, he's suddenly developed a runny nose along with some of the other indications listed, you may have cause for concern. If you simply confront him with your concerns, and even if you have hard evidence that there's a problem, he'll probably deny it. ("That's not my hash pipe; I'm just keeping it for a friend.") But if you really think there's a problem, even if he continues to deny it, you need to get help— from your doctor, a therapist, or both. Drug abuse is too serious an issue for parents to fix on their own.

Peer Orientation Means Peer Pressure

Your teen should absolutely relate to his peers. He should have friends, privacy, and a life of his own separate from yours. That said, you do want his strongest and primary attachment to be to you. Not in terms of time spent together, but in terms of the strength of your bond.

Whether the issue is drugs, alcohol, sex, or dieting, the more kids are oriented toward their peers, the more they'll feel pressured to conform. Sometimes that's okay, but there are times when they're pushed toward behavior that's unacceptable or dangerous. The most powerful protection we can give our kids to combat those pressures is to make them understand how much we love and value them.

In his book *In the Realm of Hungry Ghosts*, Gabor Maté talks about addiction in all its forms, and concludes that the most effective defense against it is the presence of a nurturing and consistent caregiver. Conversely, the greatest risk occurs when children feel detached from their caregivers and try not only to get that sense of connection from their peers, but also to medicate away their negative feelings. As Maté puts it, "Love is the drug kids need." Our job as parents is to make sure we're drugging our kids with oxytocin and the endorphins that give them a natural "high." The more we mirror and connect, the more we influence the development of their attachment circuitry in positive ways. And the more those reward chemicals are released into their bloodstream, the more bonded to us they'll feel, the more they'll want to please us, and the more being around us will please them.

As a culture we've more or less accepted that it's normal for adolescents to be grumpy, pull away, and not want to talk to us. I suspect that those are really attachment behaviors, and that the more we ignore them the more frayed the bond between us will become and the more oriented they'll be toward their peers. At the same time, the more attached they are to us, the less their sense of self will depend on the opinions of their peers.

Many adolescents experiment with drugs and alcohol, but those who are the healthiest and most closely connected to their parents are the ones most likely to "take it or leave it." A study conducted at the University of Minnesota and published in the *Journal of the American Medical Association* in 1997 underlines the point: it showed that parent/family connectedness tends to protect children against early initiation of sex as well as cigarette and alcohol use.

Kids with a solid parental bond hold their parents in their consciousness when there are decisions to be made. They care about what you'd think of their course of action and they don't want to hurt you. They're the ones who are likely to say to themselves, *I know this is stupid; I shouldn't be doing this; I need to get out of here.* Still, it can be difficult in social situations for kids to "just say no." By the time they reach their mid-teens (or, unfortunately, even younger these days), they've probably been to parties where other kids are drinking. If they just stop going to parties or hanging out with their friends they can become socially isolated, but you can help them navigate better in uncomfortable situations by giving them an out. You might, for example, arrange a secret code in advance to call your teen at a certain time and ask if he's having fun. If he answers "Yeah, I'm having fun," great, things are going well. But if he says, "Mom, are you serious? C'mon!" it means, *You need to get me out of here.* Cooperative action like this allows your kid to save face while also making you a partner in his decision-making.

Kids Want You to Be the Parent

Pushing boundaries is normal for teens, just as it is for younger children, but there's a difference between pushing boundaries and behaviors that, if left uncorrected, could have consequences that will haunt both you and your child for years to come. It makes sense for you to impose consequences now rather than stand back and allow your child to pay a much higher price in the future.

Your teen wants you to intervene, no matter how much he may be trying to hide it from you. He may bark like a dog to seem big and fierce, but if you remain calm and the consequence you imposed is fair, natural, and reasonable, he'll go away for a bit, reflect on his behavior, and come back with a genuine apology. The more you back off the less connected he'll feel, and the more that perceived lack of attachment will be reflected in his behavior. The less loved he feels the less lovable he will act. That push/pull, I love you/I hate you behavior is a signal that your child is feeling disconnected. Instead of stepping away and leaving him to his own devices, you need to ramp up the mirroring and connecting more than ever. It's his job to start detaching from you; it's your job to let him know that you understand what's going on, you love him, and he'll always be connected to you.

There will be moments when she infuriates you, but it doesn't have to be that way most of the time. Some kids make it harder than others—just as some adults make it harder than others for you to like them. Even in the same family, one child may know exactly how to push your buttons, and your reactions to her will be different from your reactions to your other kids. That's normal. But the more you're able to mirror and contain without flying off the handle or throwing up your hands and walking away, the more she'll feel that all-important tension on the rope and the less she'll need to let go of her end. As a general rule, you can assume that the child with whom you least feel like mirroring is the one who needs it the most!

SIX

Behaviors That Drive Parents Nuts

Because of that undeveloped frontal lobe, adolescents and teens are natural procrastinators. This is one of the classic behaviors that tend to drive parents nuts. It inevitably leads to nagging and stress for everyone involved.

Late, Late, Late

Let's say your daughter has to be at school by nine a.m. and it's now five minutes to nine. In her mind she isn't late—even though she knows it's going to take her at least fifteen minutes to get there. She doesn't want to be late. It's not her intention to be late. And on some level she even knows that she should have left fifteen minutes ago.

Research on the teenage brain has shown that it's natural for teens to go to bed late (around midnight) and wake up at eleven or twelve the next day. Of course that schedule doesn't work very well in the real world, and it leads to huge battles between parents and teens when it's time to get up in the morning.

Another thing to keep in mind is that not everyone perceives time the same way. Some of us are always early, and some of us—I can tell you from personal experience—just tend to be late. We don't mean to be late, but the items on our daily agenda just seem to take more time than we expected. If your teen is one of the late ones, try to explain that his perception of time may be a bit off. You might say, "I've noticed that every time you leave when you think you should, you wind up being late. And I know you don't really want to be late. So how about this? From now on, leave when you think it's fifteen minutes too early. Then you'll be on time. I know that's not going to be easy. It's not always easy for me either, but if you do it, you'll see, you're going to get to school [or wherever] on time."

Of course, it will likely take more than one discussion to achieve the desired result. And it's unbelievably frustrating when your teen won't get out of bed and you know he's going to be late for school. You're agitated. Meanwhile, he ignores you, rolls over, and pulls the sheets over his head. The more relaxed he is about it, the more maddening it is. It's an ugly scene and a horrible way to start the day. And if you drive him to school, as many parents do these days, you may be even more upset because you too are going to be late. So your inclination is to yell at him once he's in the car, loudly reminding him of all the other times he's been late. Well, stop for a minute: imagine how you'd feel if you were in a hurry and someone was yelling at you like that. So what should you do? As always: mirror, present the problem, find a solution.

I believe you should always give the child a chance to alter his behavior, but it has to be for the right reasons if the change is going to be long-lasting. By the time they're in their teens, kids need to be given some control over their lives. So I always recommend that parents make a pact with their tardy teen. Choose a moment when you're both relaxed and *not rushing*. Using the CALM technique, explain that you know what you've done in the past isn't working, and outline what you expect of him in the future. The conversation might go something like this: "You know, I've been thinking about it, and I've been horrible. I'm yelling at you every morning. I get upset when you're late and then I do all the wrong things. It's not helping at all. You're still late, and we aren't getting along very well. We need to do something to make it better. So for the next week I'm going to leave you alone. I promise not to nag. I won't say anything. I want you to have the chance to figure this out on your own. But if I don't see any improvement, if you're still consistently late by the end of the week, you might be telling me with words that you don't want me to bug you but you'll be telling me with your behavior that you need my help, and that help is going to come in the form of a consequence to give your brain some motivation. It will be your choice entirely. If you don't want the consequence, you'll have to make sure you get out the door on time."

If you normally drive your child to school, you might say, "I told you I'd leave you alone for a week, and I will. But I need to get to work on time, so if you aren't ready when I need to leave, you'll have to get there on your own." Or, if he already gets himself to school, you'll just need to sit back, bite the bullet, and tell yourself that even if he misses his first class for a week, it won't be the end of the world. Sometimes you just have to take a gamble and let your kid suffer the consequences—assuming they aren't dangerous. Our tendency is to do just the opposite. When they were little we might have run after them waving their lunch box as the school bus drove off. Now that they're older we're more likely to get out the car keys and drive them to school—even if that means we're going to be late for work. But in this case, you just have to back off and see what happens.

Maybe it will work and he'll arrive on time, in which case you'll both be pleasantly surprised. And if it doesn't, if you're getting calls or emails from the school telling you that your son has missed or has been late for his first class, when the trial period is over you can say, "Look, we tried it. I promised I wouldn't nag you and I didn't. You thought you could do this on your own, but it's obviously harder than you thought. If you keep it up it's going to affect your grades and I wouldn't be a good parent if I allowed that to happen. You want to do it differently, but it's not working. And I love you enough for you to be mad at me about this." The key is *not* to do this in a way that says to your teen, "I told you so! I knew this was never going to work!" If you present it in a respectful way, you'll find that he'll be willing to work with you.

First, you mirror again. "You know, it's hard, and people just don't get it. In your head it seems like it's working, but then you find yourself being late and you're mad at yourself and embarrassed. That doesn't mean you're a bad person. It just means that this behavior is more tightly wired into your brain than you thought. So here's how I'm going to help you. If you're not ready by [whatever time he needs to leave for school—or you need to leave for work] I'm going to leave without you. If you're late more than [you decide; I'd say twice in a week] you'll lose your computer privileges after [you pick the time] or you'll have to go to bed earlier [or you can't go out on the weekend or whatever you know will be meaningful for your own child], because that's a privilege you get for being responsible and you'll be showing me that you're not a responsible teenager. It's your choice. If you want to be treated like an adult, if you want freedom and responsibility, you have to demonstrate that you're responsible." Don't threaten, don't raise your voice. Just put it out there the way it is.

You can tell him you'll help by knocking on his door, but listen to what your own child says about the way he prefers to be awakened. Most kids have very specific ideas about that, and if you irritate them, you certainly won't be helping. You need to resist the urge to help every five minutes, and you need to understand that he may not wake up the way you do or the way you think he should. The result is what's important, not how it's achieved.

One client told me that if she didn't nag her daughter Sarah to get ready and then drive her to school, she simply wouldn't go. That is, in fact, your teen's ace in the hole. It's what most parents fear when I explain this technique, and in some instances it might be true. But most kids *will* go to school, and you need to be brave enough to call their bluff. School is a huge part of every teen's life, and most of them really want to go. But even if your child doesn't go to school for a day or two, is that really the end of the world? And if the behavior does become a pattern, you may have to help your teen by coming up with a consequence, as long as it's fair and reasonable. You might, for example, suspend some (or in extreme cases all) screen privileges so that playing games online, texting friends, and otherwise amusing herself is no longer an option. And when you do impose these consequences, make sure your teen understands that they are in fact privileges, not rights, and if other important responsibilities aren't taken care of, they can and should be suspended. And, as I discussed in Chapter Four, don't ever take anything away when you're in the heat of a battle. You don't ever want to get into a physical tug of war with a teen. Let her know in advance what the consequence will be, and then take it away while she's sleeping or out of the house.

In this case Sarah was constantly being rude and even verbally abusive toward her mother, who was the disciplinarian in the family, always nagging her to do her homework or go to bed or get up or get ready while Dad sat back and let them duke it out. This dynamic was driving a wedge between the parents, polarizing the family.

As it happened, when the issue came up it was already the end of the school year; exams were over, and there was just a week or so to go before summer vacation. I told Sarah's mother to stop trying to make her do anything. Instead, I put her on a regimen of soft parenting—mirroring and connecting as much as she could while ignoring everything else because her relationship with her daughter was not, at that point, strong enough to tolerate any more battles. If Sarah skipped school in the last few days of term, it wasn't going to be a tragedy. And maybe if Mom stepped back, Dad would step up and do some of the hard stuff. But even if he didn't, Sarah's mother would be strengthening the bond between them so that, come fall, Sarah would be better able to tolerate the containing. Or, as often happens, some of those unwanted behaviors would simply disappear as her relationship with her mother improved.

The thing is, our nagging (or as we would prefer to call it, "reminding") them to do things doesn't really help our kids develop their own sense of time. In fact, it can have the opposite effect. There's a story my husband loves to tell about when he was a kid and his father was continually trying to get him to mow the lawn. The nagging had been going on for so long that my husband had developed a finely honed sense of the exact tone of voice his dad would use when he really meant it. One day his mother said, "Why don't you just for once mow the lawn without your father's having to yell at you?" And my husband's response was, "It's okay, Dad will let me know when it's time." What he was actually saying was that he'd know when his father really, truly meant what he said. In other words, he could tell when he'd pushed his father to the limit of his patience.

That kind of ongoing battle is exhausting for parents, and it doesn't help their teens learn how to self-motivate. We need to mean what we say and stick to it. The more we do this the more they'll believe us, and the less often we'll find ourselves purple in the face and screaming.

By following the plan I set out above you're setting up a kind of protective umbrella. You're saying to your child, "I'm going to give you enough rope to succeed or fail on your own, but I'm not going to let you fall too far." Or, to alter the metaphor slightly, you're providing a safety net. If the net is just an inch under his feet, he'll take too many risks; if it's forty feet down, that might be too scary. You need to slowly lower the net as he shows you he can handle more freedom. By doing that you're demonstrating respect for your teen as an emerging adult.

The same plan works for homework, room-cleaning, or any other responsible behavior you're trying to instill or reinforce. Teens appreciate it because it gives them some sense of control. If they do it on their own, they're changing internally, and that's great. Sometimes they can't do it on their own, and if you're kind and nurturing in the way you help them, they'll be fine with that. If, on the other hand, you're screaming and lecturing and saying "I told you so," you'll be blowing a great opportunity for both of you.

Procrastination: Waiting for the Perfect Moment

Homework, and studying in general, are probably the biggest issues causing kids to procrastinate and parents to explode. Your teen keeps putting it off because he'd rather be doing something else, and you get more and more upset because you know he's got to get it done. So you hover and nag, plead and wheedle, driving both yourself and your kid totally crazy. But you must first understand that your teen does intend to do his homework—sometime—when that perfect homework moment presents itself. He truly believes that the moment will arrive when he'll suddenly, spontaneously *feel* like doing it.

Boys in particular (although girls aren't totally immune) seem to go into some kind of fugue state that makes it difficult for them to remain conscious of the passage of time. If you're the parent of a teenage boy, this will probably sound familiar to you. You find your son glued to his video game as usual. You say, "Okay, ten more minutes and then you need to start your homework." "Oh yeah, sure, absolutely, no problem." So you walk away. But when you come back an hour later he's still there in front of the computer. "So," you say. "Have you finished your homework already?" "Huh?" "Your homework, remember, you were supposed to go do it an hour ago." And you can practically see him mentally smacking himself in the head as he says, "Oh no! I'll do it in a minute. Sorry, I forgot."

This may seem impossible to you, but for these kids five minutes turns into an hour and they have no idea how much time has passed. One young client described it to me this way: "I know I have a tendency to drift off and just start daydreaming in class, so this day I decided that I was absolutely going to stay focused and listen. I swear, that was my intention. So I walked into class and stared at the teacher, and the next thing I knew the bell was ringing and I had absolutely no idea what she'd been talking about or how so much time could have passed." Even he was amazed something like that could have happened.

How can you help a teen understand that the perfect homework moment never comes? One technique I often recommend is to talk to him about his "now" self and his "future" self. Explain that you totally understand that his now self believes it's a really good idea to play that video game and that he's absolutely positive the optimal moment for beginning his homework will come—but it won't. It didn't the last time he thought it would, or the time before that, and it isn't going to happen this time either. And because it's not coming, his future self is going to suffer, either by staying up really late or by failing a test. And it's going to be his future self that opens the envelope containing the report card with the disappointing grades.

Since procrastination is such a hot-button issue for so many parents, here's an example of how we typically talk to our teens about homework and studying, followed by an example of how to mirror and CALM them. The scenario is this: Jonah has just received his report card. His grades are mediocre and you know he can do better. He keeps telling you that he doesn't have any homework or that he did it all in school, and you know that doesn't make sense. So, here's the way you may have been dealing with the issue up to now:

> PARENT: You know, Jonah, you keep saying you don't have any homework and that just doesn't make sense to me.
>
> JONAH: What do you mean? I told you, I did it in school. And anyway, Ms. Bostwick doesn't give very much homework.
>
> PARENT: Okay then, I'm going to call the school. I just don't understand this. And even if you don't have any homework you should be using that time to review what you did in class.
>
> JONAH: What do you mean? That's ridiculous. That sucks! Nobody's parents make them do that.
>
> PARENT: How are you ever going to get anywhere in life? How are you ever going to learn …

The conversation winds up with Jonah saying something like "You hate me! You never make my sister do that!" To which you may—rightly—respond: "Well maybe that's because your sister does her homework!" At which point you walk away frustrated and Jonah stomps off muttering about how mean and what a jerk you are.

So how can you change the scenario? Using the CALM technique, you might say something like this:

> PARENT, MIRRORING: Hey, Jonah, what are you watching?
>
> JONAH: It's a rerun of Buffy the Vampire Slayer.

PARENT: Oh, that's the episode where ... [and give some detail
from the show; or, if you have no idea what the show is
about:] You look like you're really into that program. Isn't
that the one where ...? [Ask in an interested but somewhat
neutral way, and try not to sound like a preschool teacher.
Kids hate that.]

You'll need to make two or three statements here, but watch to
make sure your teen isn't getting annoyed. If he's happy to talk
about it, ask a question related to the program. If he seems annoyed,
mirror that: "I'm sorry. You love this show and I'm wrecking the
moment for you." Then walk away for a few minutes. At this point
he might feel bad about having acted annoyed, and when you do
come back he may be inclined to be more accommodating. (If you
had walked away ranting, he'd be happy he's upset you.)

When you do come back, you need to present the problem
while staying completely neutral:

PARENT: You know, I'm kind of wondering when you're going to
be doing your homework.
JONAH: Oh, I don't have any.
PARENT: That certainly makes your life a lot easier. You have
more time to do what you want. That's a great feeling, but I'm
kind of struggling with what you're telling me because it isn't
what most kids seem to be experiencing. Can you help me
understand?
JONAH: Well, it's because I do it at school.
PARENT: Oh, so you have it worked out where you can get your
homework done in school.
JONAH: Yup.
PARENT: That sounds reasonable, and it sounds like it should work.
I understand why you like that plan, except that, looking at

your report card, it doesn't seem to be working so well because I know you can do much better than these marks.

JONAH: Those marks are fine. There's nothing wrong with those grades.

PARENT: Hmm, this is a hard one because you feel okay about it but I'm struggling with the fact that I know you have the potential to do much better. I know that with just a little more effort you'd be really proud of your marks and not just okay with them. So how about doing some review?

JONAH: That's ridiculous. Why would I do that if I don't have to?

PARENT: I know. I get that no one wants to do work they don't have to do. But it's a way to burn the stuff into your brain now so that when you study later most of it will already be there. You need to think about that, and we need to come up with something that works better for us so that I stop nagging you so much.

Then walk away and let him think about it. I know that at this point many of you may be thinking, *Why should I tiptoe around my kid? If I tell him to do something, he should do it.* But if you've had that conversation more than a couple of times already and he still isn't doing any homework, you have to try a new tactic. Parenting is one of the few areas in our lives where we keep doing the same thing over and over again even though we're not seeing any positive results. If you followed a route meant to take you from point A to point B and found that it led you right back to A, you'd certainly look for a different route. By making these changes, you and your teen can chart a course to the place you want to be instead of looping back to the place you started from.

Note that this conversation doesn't have a definitive conclusion. By the time you walk away it will probably have gone on a lot longer than the first version, and it's perfectly okay to end by saying something like "Why don't you just think about it." You will have planted the seed; now you can let it germinate. A day or two later (not an hour later), you can go back and say, "You know, I really think I need to call the school just to make sure, because maybe you're missing something and there really is more to do than you think."

Alternatively, you can end your initial conversation by saying, "Why don't we just leave it this way for three weeks. Then I'll check with your teachers, and if they tell me things are improving, we'll leave things the way they are."

The key point is to make sure Jonah doesn't end up angry with you. You want him to walk away from your conversation in a reflective mood. Instead of nagging and berating him, you want to get him thinking. You could even say something like, "I want you to think about how you felt when you got that report card." (And he'll probably say "I felt fine," because most kids are reluctant to admit they're at fault.) But you might press the point by asking, "Was that something you were really proud of?" To make this work, you have to be willing to put the idea out there and then give your child time to think about it before you bring it up again. Just having that nonconfrontational conversation and planting the seed in his brain will often be all that's needed for him to make the necessary changes—even though he may not come running to tell you that you were right. But if after a period of time (and you'll need to determine how long that should be) you don't see any improvement, you'll need to set a deadline and introduce a consequence.

When It's Your Issue, Not Theirs

A note of caution: It's one thing to help your teen better manage his time, but sometimes we just want our kids to do things the way we would do them. If you're one of those people who always gets things done early, it may drive you crazy that your child is a last-minute kind of person. Some people just can't buckle down to work unless they're on a deadline. If your kid is like that, you can try to create artificial deadlines for him. You might, for example, say that he needs to get his homework done or his paper written before he can go out with his friends. That sometimes works. But you also need to ask yourself this: *If he's getting it done, does it really matter that he's not doing it the way I would?* If his way of working isn't directly affecting you (except by making you nuts), it shouldn't really be a problem. It's when you're being inconvenienced (because, for example, he didn't print out his report until the last minute and the printer ran out of ink so you had to run to the store to buy a new cartridge) that you need to address it. Otherwise, it's really your issue, not his.

Helping Teens Get Motivated

For better or worse, technology has made us impatient. We've become used to accessing information more or less instantly whenever and wherever we need it. Kids no longer have to go to the library, search through a card catalog, and take down notes from documentary sources. Research now means clicking a mouse or touching a screen. One result of these developments is that many kids just don't see why they have to learn all this "stuff." Why should they cram their brains with arcane knowledge, whether it's ancient history or higher math, when the material is so easily available? When your teen asks "Why do I have to learn algebra?" it really isn't such a stupid question. If we stop to think about it, they know a lot of things we don't—such as how to use all the functions on their cellphones and how to circumvent the parental controls you've put on the computer—because those things seem relevant to them.

Of course, it's still important for teens to apply themselves in school. I sometimes explain this to kids by reminding them that whenever they learn something new they're building new pathways in their brain, and that the more pathways they have the easier it's going to be to learn the things *they* want to learn. The more things they learn, the faster they'll be able to learn other things. The connection may not always be obvious, but it's there. For example, if you play hockey, doing pushups isn't going to help you handle the puck better, but it will build muscles and strength so that you'll have more stamina on the ice. Doing algebra is like doing pushups for the brain. Algebra is really problem-solving, and the better you get at problem-solving by doing algebra, the more easily you'll be able to solve the problems *you* want to solve—like figuring out what to do when your computer freezes or how to get to the next level when you're playing a video game.

Beyond schoolwork, however, you can help kids to see how abstract concepts (like the importance of being on time or learning algebra) have practical relevance by letting them fail and take the consequences. When a teen isn't motivated, it's really we parents who are struggling—he's fine the way he is. We tend to respond to his inertia by threatening, punishing, bribing, lecturing, and begging him to change. We rant that he's never going to get into college or get a decent job. We despair that he's clearly destined to wind up homeless. And he sits there and says, "That's okay, I can live in the basement." And because we're not about to let that happen, we wind up doing his work for him. If your kid knows you won't let him fail, he'll take advantage of your concern. He'll say, "Okay, then I'll just fail!" (A classic example of threatening to cut off his nose to spite your face.) Chances are he won't let himself fail. He's just seeing how far he can push you. But even if he does fail, it won't be the end of the world.

Letting your child experience the consequences of his actions (or inaction) can be hard. None of us wants our teen to fail, but it's important that he feel that discomfort. The message you want to be sending is that when something feels bad, when it hurts, you're learning and growing. Healthy adversity is critical to brain development. If you keep on rescuing them, they'll never learn how to handle new challenges—or they'll learn much later, when it's more painful and the consequences are more serious. If you think there's going to be a perfect time to let your child fail, you're as delusional as the kid who's waiting for that perfect homework moment. Or the moment will come when you're so angry that you're reacting instead of responding. And when that happens, the lesson won't be coming from a loving place.

One of the reasons I believe it's so important for us as parents to back off from taking a hard line with our teens is that, at best, they'll be doing what we want simply because they're afraid or trying to avoid a punishment. At worst, our approach will eat away at the relationship we have with them. The more we practice mirroring and connecting the more natural it will begin to feel, until it becomes our default mode of communication. If you've been turning a great big heavy wheel in one direction it will take some effort to get it moving the other way, but once you've built up some momentum it will just keep turning on its own. Once again, when our teens feel connected to us, they'll be more likely to feel the motivation that comes from that relationship. If they do something just to avoid punishment or because you've bribed them, they won't take ownership of their behavior. In the end, your relationship—letting them know you believe in them, you'll help them, but you won't do it for them—is really all you've got.

Why Some Boys Hate to Bathe

One behavior that baffles parents and brings out the worst kind of nagging is the (to them) completely irrational reluctance their boys have to getting clean. Some adolescent boys seem to expend more energy arguing about and avoiding showering than they would if they just took one in the first place! If your teen is like this, you may be surprised to learn that the reason he doesn't care if he looks like Charles Schulz's Pig-Pen isn't very different from the reason he puts off doing homework and other chores—it just isn't important to him. It's hard to believe, but many teenage boys don't mind wearing dirty socks. They aren't bothered if their fingernails are dirty and they think it's normal to be hot, sweaty, and smelly. They don't notice the same things girls do, and the things they don't notice don't exist for them. Because their teenage brain isn't very good at stepping back and sharing another person's perspective, they can't wrap their mind around the idea that they need to take other people's perceptions into account.

In some cases, the different ways girls and boys view hygiene might be used to your advantage. You might point out to him that girls don't want to spend time with unwashed boys. In fact, girls generally find sitting next to a smelly guy in the lunchroom or in class to be absolutely gross. Letting him know this may work, but it may not, depending on how much he cares about girls.

But there are also other reasons why adolescent boys may not get around to showering. For one thing, they often have trouble using their cingulate system (see page 75) to transition from one activity to another. I know that may seem bizarre, but showering is a transition. To understand how they feel, just think what it's like to be really comfortable lying in bed and then listening to someone insisting that you get up, go out in the cold, and drive somewhere. And, like kids who put off doing their homework, they believe that the perfect shower moment lies somewhere in the not-too-distant future. Sometimes, however, the problem may go even deeper. Particularly when kids have struggled with ADHD or a learning disability, the steps required for showering become overwhelming.

At some point, someone may well say something that embarrasses them, and that will get them to see things differently. But if you're tired of waiting, you can also let them know that as long as they're living in your house, they need to take your feelings into account. Mirror first, then set consequences: "If you don't clean up your act, you can't watch television with us because you're smelly." Or, "If you don't shower you can't go out to dinner with the rest of the family."

If your fifteen-year-old son hasn't showered and has been wearing the same socks for three days, you're probably tired of fighting about it, and it's getting embarrassing because his hygiene reflects on you as a parent. At that point you might lose it and come out swinging: "You're disgusting. You smell and I can't stand being near you." At which point your teen probably says, "I hate you. You can't tell me what to do. I'll go live somewhere else," and so on. Or else he'll say, "I'm going to, I said I would." And you say, "That's what you say all the time." And then you start yelling about all the other stuff he doesn't do when he says he will. By then, if by some miracle he actually does get in the shower, he's already so mad at you that those feelings are going to come out later in some other behavior. And then, when you ask him to do something else, he's likely to snap at you.

So here's a more effective approach. Mirror first: "I know I'm always nagging you about showering and I don't think I've ever stopped to think about why you don't want to. There are a lot of really annoying steps. First you need to get out a towel and the soap. Then you have to take off your clothes and get the water to the right temperature. Then you're cold and you have to dry off and find clean clothes and socks and shoes and put everything on again. So is it that there are so many steps? Is it that you've got other things to do? Is it that you have a hard time stopping what you're doing and getting started on something else? Is it that you really do believe you're going to shower later when that magical shower moment presents itself?" Now, because you're calm and you're trying hard to see the situation from his point of view, he might say, "I just don't understand why I have to."

Then you say, "Okay, so for you it's not an issue. You feel fine the way you are, and here I am ordering you around. I can see why that would be annoying."

He might say, "Yeah, that's right, you're always ordering me around." Or, "I do shower." Or he'll come up with some other excuse.

Instead of arguing, at that point you need to move the discussion forward. "But here's the problem. We have to come to some kind of resolution. You have to shower. There are health reasons and there are family reasons. You have to look presentable because it's a reflection on all of us, and also, you stink! No one wants to be near you." You might ask him what someone else in the house does that really bugs him, and he might say, "Well, I hate it when Jenny sings in the morning." Then you say, "Okay, she's polluting your environment. Well, you're polluting our environment with your BO."

Or you might talk about how procrastination gets in the way of his completing tasks, which means that someone is always nagging him. Then ask, "How is being nagged all the time better than just taking the shower and not being hassled?" In this way you're helping his adolescent brain make the connections he might not yet be capable of making on his own.

After you've mirrored and explained the problem, you can hand him responsibility for resolving it. "I'm going to give you a few days to figure this out. No one's going to bother you, but if you don't make a significant improvement in X days you'll be showing us with your behavior that you can't do it on your own. There are consequences for the rest of the family when you don't shower, so there'll be consequences for you." And then lay out whatever consequence seems appropriate and will be meaningful for your particular child. At the end of the time you've given him, if he hasn't started showering, you mirror again: "This is a lot harder than we thought. It doesn't look like you're going to be able to do this. You're telling me that you need me to help you." And you deliver the consequence. Don't yell, don't get angry. You don't want your kid to walk away feeling totally demeaned and deflated.

But What If My Kid Is Just Lazy?

Many parents think their teen is procrastinating or late because she's lazy, but laziness—as well as other annoying or unacceptable patterns of behavior—is generally a symptom of something else.

A kid may be lazy because whatever you want her to do doesn't seem relevant to her or because you haven't been setting the limits that would teach her to change. Behavior hangs around if it can. We as parents need to make sure we're not enabling it. For example, if we get tired of waiting for our kid to do what we ask and do it for her, what she learns is that she just has to out-wait us. As always, it's important to be an observer of yourself. Is that the scenario in your home?

Procrastination, however, is sometimes in the eye of the beholder. Not everyone works on the same schedule. If our teen meets her deadlines consistently, there may be no good reason to question how she does it. Let's say your kid has an assignment to hand in on Monday: to you it makes sense for her to do it at the beginning of the weekend so that she can then relax, but she leaves it for Sunday evening. To you this would be incredibly stressful, but to her it isn't. But if she gets it done on time and gets a good grade, the problem is really yours—not hers. So, if you like to get things done early and your kid leaves things to the last minute but gets them done, as far as she's concerned you're nagging about nothing.

And if she doesn't get it done, that too will help her learn. It probably took you years of trial and error to come up with your own time-management strategies, and you're no doubt thinking you can prevent your teen from making the same mistakes you did. But learning doesn't work that way. Kids need to experience failure so that they can store the emotionally charged memory for future use.

Mom, Can I Get a Tattoo?

Why would teens want to get piercings and tattoos? From a parent's point of view it's self-mutilation; from their point of view it's decoration and self-expression. The problem—particularly with tattoos—is that once you get one it's really hard, if not impossible, to get rid of. Kids, of course, can't conceive of ever wanting their tattoos to be erased, but we can easily imagine them grown up in their business attire or wedding dress with some huge ugly "thing" on an exposed body part. It's the job of the not-completely-developed frontal lobe to envision a future time when circumstances are different, and that long-range, logical thinking has to compete with the much stronger, feeling part of the brain, which is telling them how much they need that tattoo right now.

Teens are always the stars of their own movie, and this makes it difficult for them to see anything from another person's point of view. But you can at least try to have that conversation with them. Again, mirroring could help. You might say something like, "It's your body and you want to express yourself. You believe that you ought to be able to make decisions about what to do with your own body," and so on. In fact, many teens feel that just about the *only* thing they can control is their own body.

Most jurisdictions require parental permission for children under a certain age to get a tattoo. If you live in one of them, you can simply refuse. Of course, your teen will probably tell you that you're mean and ruining her life, but you can mirror again about controlling one's own body and return to the theme of the now self and the future self. And if, in the end, she goes out and does it anyway, you need to make it clear that you love her anyway. You may hate what she's done, but you love her. And then get over it because it's done. There's nothing you can do about it and it isn't the end of the world. The more connected you are with your teen, the more you've been mirroring and creating those little connecting moments, the less likely it is that she'll feel the need to express herself in these ways.

Choosing Your Battles

Parenting is hard. If you initiate a zero-tolerance policy and fight over every single thing you'll be exhausted, and even more importantly you'll be putting a tremendous strain on that fragile but all-important attachment bond. You'll be perceived as mean, which in the end will undermine whatever guidance you're trying to offer. One way I've helped parents pick their battles is to use a strategy I adapted from Ross Greene's book *The Explosive Child*. Decide with your teen what's *okay*, what's a *maybe*, and what's a *no-way* issue. So, for example, staying up late to finish a school project or having a messy room might be okay. Going to a friend's house for the weekend is probably a maybe, depending on the circumstances, and driving with someone you don't know or going to a party where there's no adult supervision would, depending on the age and maturity of your child, be a no-way. It all depends on what's most important to you as a parent, on being firm and fair, and, of course, on what you feel you need to do to keep your teen safe.

You'll need to set up a quiet time to sit down with your partner or spouse, make a list of the most common issues you have with your teen, and determine which ones you're able to let go (those that are okay), which ones you'll have to decide on a case-by-case basis (the maybes), and which ones are never going to be okay (the no-ways). Once you've made the list, you can jointly present it to your teen. Let him be part of the conversation, and work with him to come up with appropriate consequences for engaging in the no-way behaviors or for doing something that might have been a maybe but turned into a no-way. Ask him what he thinks is fair. Let him know that the more he shows you he's trustworthy the more you might be able to turn the maybes into okays.

Making these determinations with his input allows your teen to know what your answer is going to be before he even asks. It also means that your "theme songs" (the sometimes too-automatic answers to a teenager's request) and the mood you're in won't color the way you respond. For example, if you're a mom and you had a bad experience with a boy, you may be tougher on your daughter about dating because your theme song is that boys "only want one thing." By doing that, you're projecting your experience onto hers. And if you're in a bad mood, say if you're tired or stressed, it might lead you to say no way to something that was a maybe or even an okay just a few days earlier. (Sometimes no can become the default answer.) Having a list in place can help you to avoid this kind of inconsistency.

The most difficult questions to answer, of course, are the maybes. If you're having a bad day and your kid is bugging you about a maybe, you might be inclined to say no right away just to get him off your back. But if you do a little diagnostic on yourself and realize that your own mood is affecting your response, you can step back and say something like, "You know, I really need to think about that. It may not be a yes, but if you insist on my giving you an answer this minute, it's definitely going to be a no. So give me some time, don't bug me, and I'll come back to you with my decision."

Maybes are also hard because they tend to have "ifs" attached: "Maybe you can go to your friend's house for the weekend, if ..." And the "ifs" are where you need to determine how you and your teen can work together to turn it into an okay. They're also the conditions about which your teen is most likely to give you an argument. You might, for example, decide that it would be okay if the friend's parents were going to be present, or if your teen finished all his homework, or if he agreed to phone you each day at a particular time. If he handles the maybe well and comes up with a responsible plan for making it a yes, you both win, and you can connect this responsible behavior with the positive outcome. If, on the other hand, he stomps and complains and gets nasty, he'll be turning the maybe into a no-way because of the behavioral choices he's made. This is a great way to help your teen understand the link between cause and effect—between his behavior and the outcome.

If you say no to a request and your teen reacts well—without any stomping, whining, or arguing—you might think about that and decide that you said no too quickly. You can change your mind, but only because you've rethought your own choice, never because you're giving in to nagging or other negative behavior. By changing course in this considered way, you can teach your teen how his own behavior can affect his fate while giving yourself the option of remaining flexible.

SEVEN

Lying, Bullying, and Malicious Gossip

We've already talked about some of the ways the world has become more complicated and stressful than it was when we were growing up. There are indications that many kids have come to feel both more entitled and less empathic than those of generations past. Consequently, their "social health" and interpersonal relationships are not as robust as they could or should be.

The most effective way you can ensure that your child is an empathic and resilient teen is to practice the mirroring and correcting that will strengthen not only his bond with you but also the bonds he forms and maintains with others outside your home.

That said, you can't be a parent to all the children in the world, and you can't ensure that your child won't have to deal with painful social problems such as lying, bullying, and hurtful gossip. And once again, it's the mirroring and connecting you do at home that will protect your teens from being seriously wounded by the slings and arrows that may come their way outside.

"Liar, Liar, Pants on Fire"

Maybe you remember that taunting little refrain from when you were a kid. But the fact is that kids' peers often don't call them on their lies.

One young client told me about a classmate who'd been telling all her friends that she spent every weekend at her family's home in Brazil. She probably did it to make herself seem important. All the kids knew it wasn't true, but instead of letting her know that they knew, they just made fun of her behind her back.

My older daughter, Zoë, once did call a classmate on a lie. They were chatting and she happened to pat him on the back. Maybe he was just embarrassed to have a girl touch him, I don't know. But he screamed, "Owww! That hurts!" When Zoë looked surprised and said, "What do you mean it hurts? I hardly touched you," he told her that he had a bad sunburn. Zoë's response to that was "A sunburn? It's February and you haven't missed any school." His answer? "Well, it was a very bad one."

And sometimes kids just lie impulsively. Kimberly, another client of mine, raised her hand in class one day and heard herself saying that she'd spent the summer in Scotland; she had never been to Scotland in her life. Kimberly lied a lot, and the other kids at school were starting to avoid her. When she told me about this incident she said, "I just heard the words coming out of my mouth. I have no idea why I said that." She eventually confessed to her friends that she had lied, said she wasn't going to do it anymore, and told them that if they caught her in a lie they should call her on it.

Why Teens Lie

All teens lie to some degree—in fact we all lie from time to time. That's normal. No matter how bonded they are to you or how great or how honest they are, few if any kids will never, ever lie. But most kids *are* kinda, sorta, mostly honest, and how you react to the lies they do tell can help turn them into a better or worse liar, one who lies more or less.

Many of the reasons kids lie aren't very different from the reasons we lie as adults. We might lie to a friend about having other plans because we don't want to hurt her feelings. We might buy a child ticket for the movies when we know our kid is too old—or a senior ticket for ourselves when we're too young. We all tell social lies, and our children know it, so we can't just sit them down and say it's wrong to lie, period. We really need to talk about degrees of lying and how complicated it can become.

Interestingly, kids with nonverbal learning disabilities and those with Asperger's syndrome are often the least likely to lie because they can have a hard time with the concept that there are right and wrong or good and bad reasons to lie. They may be so rule-bound that for them a lie is a lie. You might say to your kid, "Grandma's coming and she dyed her hair blue; just tell her it looks nice." Your kid might refuse because she just can't see why she should lie. To her, the moral universe is black and white.

Gifted and highly verbal kids, on the other hand, may tell the most elaborate tales because they revel in drama and have huge imaginations. This might be the kid who moans and clutches his leg when he falls on the baseball field and misses the catch. Or it might be the kid who bursts into tears after a test because she "knows" she failed, and then gets an A.

There's a continuum of lying that may start with two individuals having different perceptions of the same incident. If the way you perceive something is different from the way someone else sees it, neither of you is actually lying. Let's say you and your child get into an argument because of something he said. His perception may be that he was just minding his own business when you came at him and started yelling. Your side of the story may be that he was rude to you. But he didn't think what he said was especially rude.

Then there's social lying, which might mean telling Grandma her hair looks great because you know she loves it even if you don't. We sometimes lie to protect another person's feelings or to please ourselves without causing pain. Another example is making up a story to cancel a plan we've made because something else we'd rather do has come along.

Nasty lying sits at the other end of the continuum. Telling an untruth about another person and blaming someone else for something that's your fault are examples of nasty lies.

Very often, however, kids lie to get around us or to get out of trouble.

Top Ten Lies Kids Tell Their Parents

(With thanks to the teenagers who talked to me about this and were so honest about lying.)

1. I did all my homework at school.
2. Ms. So-and-So never gives any homework.
3. We had a substitute teacher today and she let us all go home early.
4. Josh's father is definitely going to be home for the party.
5. I'm sleeping over at Melissa's house.
6. Those aren't my cigarettes/drugs. I'm keeping them for my friend.

7. Jordan's dad will be driving us.
8. Of course I'm still a virgin.
9. I only had a sip.
10. The subway got stuck and my phone didn't work underground.

As parents, we need to be aware that we may inadvertently encourage our teens to lie. We do that when we try to contain behavior and impose consequences without first connecting. We do it when we're so focused on our own agenda that we fail to remember what we did when we were young and set consequences that are out of balance with the transgression. That's when our teen will tell us she's sleeping over at a girlfriend's house when she's really going to a party where there's going to be alcohol. We need to build a solid enough connection with our kids that they know (because we've proved to them) that if they tell us the truth, whatever it is, we're not going to freak out. Otherwise, we're just training them to become better liars. You can't force someone to tell the truth, and the more you demand or threaten your teen with consequences the more she'll hold on to the lie.

Two things parents tend to do that drives kids to lie are not showing respect for their privacy and fishing. Snooping is disrespectful, and teens are entitled to resent it. Of course, we don't call it snooping. We were "tidying up" her room and just happened to have a look in her drawer while we were putting away her socks, and we just happened to see ... That's an invasion of privacy. We'd be horrified if our kids started snooping through our stuff like that. If you really think your teen is in trouble or engaging in dangerous behaviors, you need to talk to him about it. You can certainly make it clear to him that as long as he's living under your roof you need to know what he's doing. And you can also assure him upfront that you're going to be watching him closely. Sneaking into his room to spy on him, however, isn't going to solve the problem; it's just going to drive him to hide things more ingeniously.

Parents tend to fish a lot in conversation with their adolescents: "So, where did you go? Who was there? What did you do?" These random interrogations only make them shut down, and if you keep at it long enough they'll make something up just to get you off their back. By the time they're teenagers kids shouldn't have to account for every minute of their time. The better you are about showing them that you care while giving them some space, the more likely they are to open up and share what's going on in their lives.

Lying to Feel More Important

Not long ago, Mark, who's fifteen, arrived at my office huffing and puffing, regaling me with the story of how he'd been jumped by seventeen kids who tried to beat him up and steal his iPod, and how somehow he'd fought them all off and got away with the iPod intact. It was such a great story, and Mark told it in such detail, that for a second he almost had me convinced. But of course I knew it couldn't be true. Nevertheless, I'm a therapist, right? So I couldn't just say, "Oh, c'mon, seventeen attackers? And you expect me to believe that?" So what I said was "Wow, somehow you found a way, something inside you let you fight off all those kids, and not only did you fight them off but you actually came away with your iPod!"

As I was mirroring the story back to him, I could see from the look on his face that he must have been thinking, *Well, that sounds ridiculous.* When people lie and are challenged on it, they go into fight-or-flight mode, become defensive, and further invest in the lie. They try desperately to sound credible but forget to consider how their story really sounds. After Mark listened to my recap of his story, he amended it: "Well, it wasn't really seventeen kids beating me up. It was just one kid, but the others were all standing around and watching." To which I responded, "But still, someone was beating you up and you managed to keep your iPod!" At which point he looked at me again and said, "Well, the actual truth is there was one kid and he beat me up and stole my iPod." At that point, my response was "So the first story you told me was really what you wished had happened. You wished you were that powerful." And that really helped him open up and even to cry about it.

But why lie in the first place? I can't say for sure, but Mark is a dramatic kid who likes to tell big stories. Maybe he felt he'd been humiliated and needed to overcome that feeling by inviting my admiration. The point is that if I had flat-out called him on his lie, he probably would have dug in his heels and become more invested in it. When adults confront their teens about lies they tend to make it a full-frontal attack, which just puts kids on the defensive. They get so wrapped up in their lie that they start believing it themselves, and when you don't believe them they get just as upset as they do when they're telling the truth.

I gave Mark an out. I made the conversation safe by allowing him to realize that if he told the truth I wasn't going to be judgmental. I wasn't going to yell at him or mock him or otherwise embarrass him for coming clean. In this case, and in any instance where we think a child is lying, we need to find a way to convince them that they'll benefit more from telling the truth than from insisting on the lie.

Years ago, when I was a social worker, I got called to a school because a girl's parents had both died within the previous forty-eight hours. Her mother had been in a terrible accident, and when she died after being in the hospital on life support, her father had a fatal heart attack.

When I got to the school the girl was in the principal's office, sobbing. I wondered why she'd come to school in the first place. Something didn't ring true, but of course I couldn't just confront the sobbing girl and accuse her of lying. So I called her house, and her father answered the phone. Both he and her mother were very much alive.

Behind this Academy Award performance was undoubtedly a desperate bid for attention, which indicated some underlying problem that needed to be addressed. Another child in her class really had lost a parent just a couple of weeks earlier, and both her peers and her teachers had naturally been sympathetic and supportive. Having witnessed that, the girl may have been seeking the same kind of validation. Behavior is a form of communication, and so it's important to look for its underlying causes, stressors, or issues.

As adults, we wonder of course what the girl could have been thinking. Did she really believe she'd get away with it? As a teenager, however, she wasn't thinking that far ahead. Her now self needed the attention. If she thought ahead at all, she probably figured that her future self could deal with the consequences later.

When kids feel loved they feel good about themselves, which makes them more resilient. They don't need to make themselves feel more important. It's our job as parents to let our children know that they are indeed "good enough," and we do that throughout their lives by mirroring and connecting. But when they do tell lies we also need to let them know not only that we are aware of what they're doing, but also that lying is unacceptable.

Getting that message across can be difficult when a kid is so invested in his story he isn't even listening to what he's saying. One strategy is to mirror back, as I did with my client Mark. Or, if the teen is so caught up in the moment that he can't hear you mirror, you might say something like, "You know, I love you and I want to believe everything you say. But I'm having a little trouble with this one. So I'm going to go away and I want you to think about it and come back and tell me if there's anything you left out or want to change or add." What you don't want to do is confront him, since once he's committed to the lie he'll be just as upset if you don't believe him as he would be if he were telling the truth. And when he does come back with the truth, you need to put your own agenda aside and stop yourself from saying something like "I knew it!" or imposing a consequence. What he needs to understand in that moment is that he'll always be rewarded for telling the truth.

If you impose a consequence for lying once your child has told you the truth, he won't feel bad about having lied; he'll feel bad about telling the truth. He'll perceive the consequence as an injury and become a more inventive liar.

If your teen has a history of lying, you need to mirror first and then follow up with a conversation about trust. You might begin by saying something like, "I can't imagine how awful it would be to have someone look right at you and not believe what you're telling them. That's an awful feeling and I feel terrible that you have to go through it. I was so happy last week when you told me X and it turned out to be true. That must make it even more frustrating when I don't believe you. But the truth is, there've been many times when I believed what you told me and it turned out not to be true. So I really have to check, for my own sake and for yours." With kids who are chronic liars, you need to get to the point where you check up on whatever they're telling you. Let them know that you have to do this until you see the pattern shifting and they're telling the truth more often than they're lying. But you also need to mirror first, stay neutral, and if you feel like yelling, bite your tongue.

And you also need to maintain some perspective. Many of us, if we catch our child in a lie, immediately blame ourselves and jump to the conclusion that we've failed as parents. The reality may not be so dire. Teens aren't always truthful partly because they have their own world we're not privy to, and there is a difference between lying and simply being private. If your child exhibits a pattern of lying in many different situations, you certainly need to deal with the problem. But if he or she is telling the occasional social lie, you need to think about how often you did that yourself (and maybe still do) without falling into the category of pathological liar.

Bullying and Gossip in the Twenty-first Century

When they're not lying to get out of trouble, most kids lie primarily because they're having a hard time socially and think the lie will raise their status and make them more popular. Of course, this rarely works. Instead, it tends to result in the teen's being bullied or ostracized or becoming the object of malicious gossip.

Certainly some old-fashioned sorts of bullying are still going on. But kids are becoming a lot more clever and more sophisticated in *how* they bully. And while boys used to be more physical and girls more sneakily psychological in the ways they bullied, the sexes now seem to be learning and adopting techniques from one another.

Data is inconclusive, but many parents and professionals believe girls are becoming more socially aggressive and violent. The perception, even among the teens I talk to, is that girls are becoming more physically assertive. Some particularly horrible examples of this have even been reported in the media. One incident I know about personally occurred when ninth graders from various middle schools were funneled into one feeder high school. A girl—we'll call her Stacy—had been going out with a boy from one of the middle schools, and that boy encountered another girl—let's call her Meredith—whom he knew from his previous school. She ran up to him in the hall, hugged him, and asked how his summer had been— perfectly normal behavior for two kids who hadn't seen each other all summer. Stacy, however, didn't take kindly to this display of affection and started to scream in front of everyone that Meredith was trying to steal her boyfriend. For the next several days Stacy continued to taunt Meredith every time they passed in the hallway, calling her a man stealer and hissing "I'm going to get you" under her breath. When another student asked Meredith if she was afraid, Meredith said, "Not really. I'm a second-degree black belt in karate so I'm not that scared." That somehow got back to Stacy, who took it as a threat. As Meredith was leaving school the next day Stacy followed her, screaming, and the minute they stepped off school property she literally jumped on Meredith's back, threw her to the ground, and started scratching at her face. A couple of older kids finally got them separated, and Meredith went running back into the school. Stacy got a five-day suspension, and the matter was then handed over to the police.

Thankfully, this kind of behavior is still less common among girls than the "mean girls" form of social ostracism. But another emerging problem is cyber bullying. We've already seen how preoc-cupied kids have become with the social minutiae of their lives and how text messaging and social networking can play into the problem of cyber bullying, but you may not be aware of the enormous impact these technologies have on your children.

Facebook and other social networking sites can serve many positive purposes. They're the primary ways kids stay in touch and make plans these days—the same way that, back in the dark ages, we used the telephone. They give isolated or awkward teens an opportunity to connect with others. And teens who have difficulty interacting face to face can take their time and think about responses in a way they can't in the course of a live conversation. But those same sites also provide opportunities for people to write anything they want on someone else's "wall," where anyone can read it and where the writer remains anonymous. People can also post anonymous comments where only the person whose page it is can read them. While I certainly don't advocate anyone's refusing to allow their teen to join Facebook or any other social network, as parents we really need to appreciate their potential effects—on girls in particular. For some kids, being the recipient of five anonymous messages saying they're annoying may hurt, but it may also make them stop and think, Hey, maybe I am annoying. Maybe I should try and do something about that. For others, however, those same messages can be absolutely devastating and have no beneficial effect at all.

Even in the best of circumstances, girls worry constantly about their social status. They fuss and obsess about the subtle nuances of every message and posting. They're continually trying to understand exactly what so-and-so meant when she texted such-and-such, or replaying every conversation to winkle out subtle meanings that may have been intended—or not. Most of us have worried at one time or another whether we should have said (or not said) something or tried to find the hidden meaning in another person's words. But for adolescents, that kind of hyper-analysis often gets taken to an entirely different level. One consequence is that it's harder for kids to live in the here and now because they're always thinking about what was or what could have been. They never have a moment when they're able to break away from the pressure of the group. They're always connected. When someone reaches out and touches them electronically, they feel the need to respond immediately and appropriately, which means that they're regularly living in a state of fight-or-flight. Years ago, we didn't all have a phone in our room, much less a cellphone. Now kids lie in their beds texting at two in the morning. The time we spent thinking while we walked to school or stared out the window of the bus is now spent texting—and expecting an instant response.

Today's teens honestly believe that if they fail to respond to even one text message their social status will crash. Many kids are actually reluctant to go away on vacation because they're afraid they'll miss something or that the circle will close and they'll be left on the outside when they get back. And sometimes it's the most popular kids who worry the most. Ridiculous as it seems to most adults, to a teenager, popularity can be one of the most serious attainments the world can offer. And it's precisely because so many teens are terrified of losing their place among the popular kids that so-called mean girls have so much power. Other kids tend to go along with them because they're afraid that if they don't, the group will turn on them. For kids who define themselves in terms of their popularity, that can be absolutely devastating.

Cyber gossip is a form of bullying, and, like all gossip and bullying, it can make the person doing it feel devilishly good. We gossip for a variety of reasons—to establish our status, to exercise power over another person, and sometimes simply because it's entertaining. Sometimes we gossip to make ourselves feel better because it can be comforting to know that someone else is worse off than we are. And kids often don't think of their conversation about others as gossip; they think they're only telling a secret to one friend who, of course, has promised never to tell.

What I say to my teenage clients is "If you wouldn't say it out loud in a crowded room, don't say it (or text it) at all." Kids seem to think that because they're sitting with their computer or their phone in the privacy of their bedroom, whatever they text or email is private. I have to explain that even if they think they're only telling their best friend, she, in a moment of weakness, might repeat it to one other person, who might then tell someone else, and that the farther the "secret" gets from its source, the less the person who hears it will care about keeping it. As soon as the words have left your teen's lips (or the moment she presses the send key on her phone or computer), she's lost control and has no idea where those words will wind up. If the wrong person picks up that tidbit of gossip, that's the responsibility of the person who first passed it on. Teens (and grownups too!) must learn to think of the computer as public space: the fact that they're using it in the privacy of their own home doesn't mean the information they exchange is private.

There's an eighteenth-century Jewish folktale about a woman who's been saying nasty things about another woman in the community and who goes to her rabbi asking for forgiveness and vowing to take back her words. The rabbi says he'll forgive her on one condition: that she cut up a feather pillow and scatter the feathers to the wind. She readily agrees, and when she's done she returns to the rabbi to ask if she's now forgiven. He says there's one more thing she must do first: go and collect all the feathers. "But that's impossible," she says. "Precisely," says the rabbi. Words, like feathers, are impossible to take back.

Boys seem to be somewhat less involved than girls in this constant chatter. Some even complain that the girls can drive them nuts with their endless texting and need for connection. There comes a time when teenage boys begin to be interested in girls, but when they do get a girlfriend, they often don't know what to do with her (both literally and figuratively). One teenager in my practice told me that his girlfriend "just wouldn't leave him alone." She was texting him every five minutes, even when they'd just been together for hours. He would drop her off at her house and the second the door closed she'd be texting him. He didn't want to break up with her, and he didn't want to turn off his phone, but he also didn't understand why she couldn't "give it a break." He was beginning to wonder whether having a girlfriend was more trouble than it was worth. In fact, many parents have told me their teenage sons increasingly report that they find girls to be extremely pushy and that they're overwhelmed by the attention.

When Teens Feel Invisible

Fear of becoming the victim of meanness in one form or another undoubtedly explains why many teenagers need to stay constantly in touch and to solidify their position within their social circle. Being the object of nasty gossip is hurtful, but sometimes being ignored can be just as bad.

You may remember the song from the musical *Chicago*, "Mr. Cellophane," about a guy who seemed to be invisible. Some teens feel that way too. Jessica, a sixteen-year-old client of mine, was a victim of that kind of treatment. She wasn't unattractive, but she also wasn't particularly assertive. She was quiet, the kind of kid who just didn't advocate for herself. She waited for people to come to her. If she called a friend proposing that they do something together, the friend didn't refuse, but other kids never took the initiative to call her. She felt overlooked, inconsequential, and out of it. She wanted to be seen. She didn't want to do anything outrageous or dramatic; she just wanted to be a part of things.

I looked at her sitting on the sofa in my office as she was describing her situation. Her knees were close together, her shoulders were hunched, her head was down, her arms were crossed, and she had a funny little smile on her face. Taken together, her posture and facial expression seemed to say, "Please don't look at me. I'm not really important." These are strong messages, even if they are nonverbal, and teens pick up on them.

Kids who are confident and popular tend to take up a lot of space because they feel entitled to be where they are, doing what they're doing. Less confident kids are often more tentative physically. With Jessica's permission we came up with a plan. I took a picture of her with her cellphone and showed it to her. Then I asked her to take up more space, to hold her head up and assume a more confident expression. When she did that, I took another picture. Finally I said, "Okay, now really take up space. Lay your arm out along the back of the sofa, pick up your head, look confident. Sit the way you think the most popular kid would sit, even if it feels dumb to you. Convey the message that you're important, that you should be sitting there, and that you're worth noticing." Then I took a third picture.

We compared the three pictures, and I asked Jessica which of those three kids she'd want to be friends with. The answer was pretty obvious. Her "homework" was to practice in front of a mirror or even videotape herself standing and walking in different ways, and to observe how the popular kids in her school held themselves either standing or walking.

Jessica had been startled by those pictures. She'd had no idea how strongly the image she'd been projecting essentially asked other kids to ignore her. I explained to Jessica that our body language tells others how we feel about ourselves, and that by changing her posture she could change the way people reacted to her. Making these changes consciously wouldn't turn her into a phony: it was a perfectly legitimate way to modify the way she felt about herself. She'd actually be changing her brain by building new neuropathways so that, over time, her new posture and sense of self would become completely natural. By walking, sitting, and carrying herself as if she were comfortable with herself, she'd be leading her brain to view herself more positively. Teens are old enough to understand these things. By explaining that they possess the ability to make these changes, you can give them a sense of control that's empowering—even life-changing—in and of itself.

Another of my teenage clients also seemed to be invisible. It wasn't that the other kids didn't like Joe; it was just that he was so quiet and self-effacing they tended not to notice or think about him. Again with his permission, we videotaped him walking the way he normally did. Then I told him to "walk as if you were the coolest celebrity on the planet." The girls call it swagger. A confident stance attracts peers and conveys a strong message that this person likes himself. When we played the video back, Joe was stunned to see the difference. With that picture in his mind he was able to work on changing his body language, and before long the other kids (especially the girls) were treating him like the stud he had become.

Helping Teens Cope with Bullying and Gossip

There's nothing more devastating to a parent than knowing his or her child is being bullied or ignored or simply doesn't have any friends. Most parents would do just about anything to "fix it." But by the time your child is an adolescent you can't very well call up another kid's parent to make a playdate or to complain that Josh or Hannah is being mean to little Erin. If your child is being bullied you could go to the school, but in most cases—unless there's actual physical abuse involved—the school can't or won't do much about it. That doesn't mean, however, that you're without options.

The first and best thing you can do is to CALM and connect and make sure your teen feels included and loved at home. By doing that you'll make him more resilient and better able to cope with whatever's going on in his life. Also, you can and should encourage him to make friends outside school—kids from the neighborhood, camp friends, or even cousins who live nearby. Research has shown that just one good, trustworthy friend is extremely protective and often enough to help kids feel safe and supported.

The worst thing you could do is nag and natter on about what he might be doing to make the other kids bully or ignore him. If your child is having a hard time outside the home, he'll probably be extra-cranky and annoying with you. You, in turn, will be extra-frustrated, and so it's especially important to check your own agenda to make sure you're giving him what he needs rather than what makes you feel better. Nor do you want to sound panicked: that would just make him even more desperate and could lead him to stop confiding in you. If your teen is having problems of his own, the last thing he needs is to take on your problem as well. And finally, you don't want to jump on him the minute he gets home from school or a social event and start quizzing him: "How did it go? Was it really bad?" What you're doing is tagging the bullying behavior so that he starts looking for the times when he's being treated badly rather than the times when things go well.

To help your child, you need to remain calm and discuss the problem objectively—after you've mirrored, of course. You can use the picture-taking technique I used with Jessica, and encourage him to study other kids' body language, almost as if he were a scientist. But again, don't push it. If he's getting annoyed, just stop. You have to take your cues from your teen's responses so that you don't overdo it and make things worse instead of better.

Here are a few more techniques you can use to help your teen gain the confidence that will ultimately change the way he or she is perceived and treated by others.

Thinking Before Texting

The danger (and allure) of text messaging is that it encourages an instant response. But it doesn't have to be that way. Suggest that the next time your teen receives an upsetting text message, she (it's more likely to be a she) not respond in the heat of the moment. Instead, you and she can discuss the message and together come up with a response that allows her to stand up for herself. The aim is to nip the text conversation in the bud, to find the text equivalent of what she'd say to the other person's face in a real-world encounter. You want to prevent an ongoing, escalating dialogue before it gets totally out of hand. If a bully (cyber or otherwise) doesn't get the response she's looking for, chances are she'll look for someone else to bother.

Also, let your teen know that if she's having a really hard time when you're not around, she can text you at any time. I do that with some of my clients and have found it to be an effective way to support them. But if you do use this technique, make sure your child understands that she can't abuse it by texting you constantly about every little thing. There's a fine line between supporting and enabling, and it's sometimes not so easy to see—especially for a teen.

Using TV as a Teaching Tool

Believe it or not, your teen can develop more social awareness and confidence by watching reality television programs with you. I've used shows in which there's a competition, alliances are formed, strategies are developed, and people are voted off. As you watch the program with your teen, you can point out what each of the players is doing and how it's affecting his or her chances of winning. You can also talk about who you think is going to get voted off and why. Point out the expressions on the faces of the other players when one of them talks too much or says something the other contestants think is stupid. This is a fantastic way to make teens aware of these important social cues. Make it a game of your own. Behaviors that are difficult to "see" in the midst of a social interaction may be easier to grasp when looked at from the position of a neutral observer.

Standing Up for Themselves

When a kid is being mistreated she needs to stand up for herself. Your child may have been told in school to just "ignore it" or "walk away." Or she may have been taught to say, "It really hurts my feelings when you ..." But that's exactly what the nasty kid wanted in the first place. Many things kids are taught in school about how to deal with bullies simply don't work in the real world. What does work is making a stand-up-for-yourself statement that cuts off the exchange while transferring the power from the bully to the victim. The statement needs to be strong but subtle: if she either over- or underreacts the social aggressor will know she has succeeded.

The meanness can be subtle, as in the comment one of my clients reported to me: "Wow, that's a really great sweater you're wearing. I bought it on sale last year." In that instance, my client's response was perfect. In a strong but neutral way she said, "That didn't really sound like a compliment. It sounded more like I was being dissed." It caught the mean girl so off guard (as was the intention) that she immediately backed off and said, "Oh, no, that's not what I meant at all." My client could have also said, "I know. I love this sweater. It's amazing that you got a good deal on it," and walked away.

The incident that awakened me to the power of stand-up-for-yourself statements occurred while I was an intern in training to be a therapist. In the Introduction to this book I talked about the training interviews during which we were watched from behind a one-way mirror and about how I'd been intimidated by one of the more experienced interns on the team. Because I felt inferior to her, I was hyper-alert to any mistake she might make. One day I was behind the mirror watching while she conducted a really great interview. Everyone was talking about what a wonderful job she was doing and I was becoming more and more jealous and upset. All I could focus on were the mistakes she was making, because that's how my brain was working. I simply didn't *want* to recognize the things she did well.

We shared an office, and when she came back after the interview I made a very catty remark—one of those insults disguised as advice. She looked at me with an expression on her face that said "Oh you poor sad little thing" and said in a perfectly level voice, "You know, I don't really need you to like or dislike my work." And then she left the room. There wasn't a hint of nastiness in her voice, just total confidence and a hint of pity for me. That was a profoundly awakening moment. I felt that she could see exactly what I was doing and that I'd made a total fool of myself. And I knew I never wanted to feel that way again. Without knowing it, she had handed over to me the secret power of standing up for yourself. It takes practice, confidence, and a whole lot of acting.

You can pass that secret power along to your child. If your teen comes to you complaining that someone is being nasty to her, take it as an opening. First, as always, you need to CALM, and then wait until she gives you some cue or clue that she's ready to move on to finding a solution. She might ask, for example, if the same thing ever happened to you. Or, if you're doing a good job of reflecting her feelings back to her, she might say, "Yeah, yeah, so what can I do about it?" One way or another you'll sense that it's time to introduce your own agenda. If she starts to get upset again, you'll know it was too soon and you can go back to mirroring until she's calm. The more you do this, the better you'll become at recognizing the moment.

When the time is right, you can explain that bullies are looking for a way to hurt you. If they succeed, they walk away stronger because they've taken some of your strength. It's a kind of energy transfer. Or to use another analogy, if someone offers you a rotten apple and you say no thank you, then the other person is stuck with the apple. The same thing holds true if someone tries to insult you. If you don't accept the insult, the other person is stuck with it.

If your teen plays video games, he'll know that there's almost always some kind of "power bar" in the corner of the screen that lets the player know how much life his character has left. Using this as an analogy, you can explain that when one person bullies another, he's appropriating some of their power. But when the bully's intended victim makes a stand-up-for-himself statement, his power bar goes up and the bully's goes down.

The best way your teen can stand up for himself is to adopt an expression and attitude that shows the insult hasn't bothered him at all and that he really thinks the other kid is either a little bit pathetic or crazy. The words he says aren't as important as his expression and tone of voice. He might say something as simple as "Oh, okay, whatever." Or, "You know, you do that a lot. What's up with that?" By making those kinds of statements, he refuses to accept the insult and turns it back on the other person. It's important to avoid sounding angry, flustered, or upset. Staying neutral or seeming bored is the key to success. And finally, after making the statement, your teen needs to walk away. It isn't easy to do this well, particularly in the moment when he really is upset, so you'll need to help him practice to get his tone and facial expression just right.

So what do you do if your kid doesn't come to you and give you that opening? Even if you're pretty sure something's wrong—and there are generally signs, such as his being extra-nasty to his siblings, withdrawing, refusing to go to school, or experiencing rapid mood changes—you don't want to confront him and start to interrogate him, because that will likely make him clam up even more. Either he'll feel attacked or he'll figure that you're already too upset to handle what he has to say. It's easy to fall into that trap, and I've done it myself, even though I should have known better.

A couple of years ago we were on a family cruise and my son was having a great time with the other teenagers on the ship. Then one evening I went back to our cabin after dinner and found him lying on his bed in the dark. He was clearly upset; obviously something had happened. I immediately started to say everything I counsel parents not to say. "What's going on? What are you doing in here? Is something wrong? Something must have happened. Tell me what it is. Can I help?" A relentless, ridiculous stream of questions was coming out of my mouth, and the more I pressed him the less he wanted to talk to me. The less he talked, the more terrible I assumed the problem must be. "You don't want to talk to me? You know people actually pay me to give them advice. Teenagers talk to me all the time, really!" It was awful! Finally I got a grip on myself and said in a neutral, matter-of-fact way, not sounding sorry for myself or sarcastic, with every ounce of sincerity I could muster, "You know, you're a great kid, and whatever happened I'm sure you'll work it out. I'm obviously driving you crazy, and I'm not going to do that anymore. Don't tell me anything. I wouldn't want to talk to someone who'd just asked me five hundred questions in a span of two minutes." And as I turned to leave, he started to tell me. He was supposed to meet a group of kids at the hot tub, and when he arrived they weren't there. He jumped to the conclusion that they'd done it on purpose, and so he returned to the cabin to brood.

I had to stop myself from saying, "That's it? Are you kidding me? Why don't you just go find them?" Instead I said, "Oh, so you thought they were your friends and things were going really well, and it feels like they planned to ditch you." After two or three statements like that, I introduced my own agenda: "I know it seems like that's what happened, but is it possible there's another explanation?" At which point he said, "I don't know, maybe." I then left him with a message of competence, letting him know that, either way, I was sure he'd be okay and that I'd be there if he needed me.

After I'd gone he went to look for them, and not surprisingly, it turned out there'd been a misunderstanding about where they were going to meet: the other kids had been waiting for him at a different hot tub.

So what you *should* do if you think there's a problem is mirror the nonverbal signals he's sending and simply say, "You know, I've been seeing changes in you and I think there must something going on. I don't know what it is, but it must be serious because you aren't eating and you aren't going out with your friends. It's got to be something really serious. I want to help and I don't want to badger you, but I want you to know that you can talk to me. I'll try my best to stay calm and hear what you have to say." And then you have to be brave enough to walk away and let him think about it.

You can say that you'll check in from time to time to make sure he's okay, but you have to leave him alone long enough to let him know you really meant what you said. Sometimes the mirroring will feel so good that he'll open up right away. But if he doesn't, you can use that time to mirror about other things and show him that you really are a good listener. And when he does share that precious information with you, don't blow it by pouncing on it and screaming, "Oh, finally you're telling me!" If you do, your kid will just say, "Oh god, I'm sorry I ever said anything!" and clam up all over again. Think of it as building up a listening account in the bank. Once your teen is satisfied that you really are listening, he'll talk. In fact, the CALM technique is so powerful and feels so good that he won't be able to help himself. Once you've earned his trust he will value your guidance. Try to stay neutral and don't be afraid to say, "You know, I really need to think about this and figure out how I can be most helpful." Remember to focus on conversational or incidental mirroring to keep the connection strong and to keep him feeling good about talking to you.

Finally, your teen might come to you with a problem that he

says his "friend" is having. Play along with this gambit (after all, it really might be about a friend). Chances are he's testing you to see how you'll react. If you stay calm, listen, and don't give the impression that he's telling you the worst thing in the world, he'll be more likely to get to the point where he's comfortable saying, "Well, you know, it's really me that happened to." Again, don't freak out and scream, "Why didn't you say that to begin with?" A more positive response would be "You know, I understand, you had to test me to see how I'd react. I hope I did a good job." You want him to know you're his partner and that you're strong enough to deal calmly and rationally with whatever is going on in his life.

Teaching Teens to Mirror

If mirroring has helped you be more connected to your teen, if you've seen how it can change her reaction to you, why not teach her how to mirror so that others will be drawn to her?

There's no reason why she too can't learn to listen and reflect another person's thoughts and concerns, just as you have. And she'll discover, as you have, that the CALM technique can make others feel so good that they'll want to be her friend and spend more time with her. Make sure she understands that this isn't "sucking up": it's all about putting herself in the other kid's shoes so that the other kid feels understood. You can teach her the technique through role-playing so that she can hear the nuances of tone and attitude and learn how to do it correctly.

Even without teaching her, however, you'll find that the more you mirror with your teen, the more she'll do it naturally. My son has gotten so good at it that I don't even notice until he says, "Hey, Mom, did you notice I was just mirroring?"

Even my five-year-old, Olivia, now does it. She'd been in class building a castle of blocks when she noticed the foot of the kid next to her was getting closer and closer to her tower. She got up to ask the teacher for help (which was in itself amazing because a year earlier she probably would have just smacked the other kid), but before the teacher could do anything, the other kid had knocked the castle over by driving his toy car up the ramp. The teacher braced herself for an explosion, but to her amazement, Olivia went up to the kid and said, "Josh, you know what? I knew you were looking at that castle and you were just dying to go up the ramp with your car and it was so hard to resist because it was such an awesome ramp and you were trying so hard and you didn't mean to knock it over ..." At which point Josh looked at her and replied, "You know what, Olivia? You're right, it was such a great castle and I didn't mean to break it and you worked so hard on it and you must be so sad ..." The teacher stood there with her mouth open listening to these perfect mirroring statements, and in the end the two kids rebuilt the castle together. No one had taught them to mirror, but the teacher had been using the technique and they had absorbed it. Your teen will too.

Bonding Works Both Ways

If we think our own teen is being mean or treating others badly, our instinct may be to punish them, but punishment rarely works. Punishment means we are intending to hurt them or make them pay for mistakes. Natural consequences work better, but will not work without connection first. One of the most powerful aspects of mirroring and connecting is that it creates change, whether your teen is the one being targeted or the one who's being mean. Either way, strengthening that deep emotional bond creates empathy and improves social skills.

EIGHT

When Teens Are Crying for Help

We seem to be hearing more and more these days about extreme behaviors like cutting and eating disorders among teens—and increasingly among preadolescents. This is scary for parents, but engaging in those behaviors is even scarier for the kids who are doing them.

These kids are letting you know that they're hurting very deeply, and/or that they're suffering because their bond with you is so threatened. They're crying out for help; they're saying *Look at me! I'm in trouble!* And no, they'll probably never say that to you outright. If you confront them they'll deny they're in difficulty with all their might. They want and need help, but they also don't want you to know how much pain they're in, so they become increasingly and incredibly secretive. I know that sounds crazy, but you need to remember that these are behavioral manifestations of emotional issues to begin with. Most teens who engage in these behaviors are feeling in some way inadequate and undeserving, and they don't want you to know that.

There is nothing to be gained by blaming yourself in this situation. You do need to ask yourself some tough questions, however, and to be honest with yourself so that you can move toward new, more effective and healthier patterns of communication.

Cutting, Bingeing, and Starving to Escape the Pain

Cutting (or burning, scratching, or puncturing) hurts! But for kids who cut, it's soothing. On the one hand it allows them to not think about other kinds of pain they may be feeling. On the other hand they may be so numb that they're not feeling anything, and cutting reminds them that they're alive. It becomes a way to substitute physical for emotional pain.

Cutting can go along with either anorexia or bulimia, because eating disorders are also an extreme reaction to emotional pain and a way for kids to regain a false sense of control over their lives. If your child has any of these issues, you need professional guidance, but the techniques in this book can also help and perhaps bring about changes more quickly.

Denial: Yours and Theirs

When kids are in that much pain, they desperately want you to know about it, and just as desperately, they don't want you to know. These mixed signals present you with a confusing and overwhelming emotional maze, and the stakes are high. You may be in denial because you can't or don't want to believe this is happening, and that makes the issue even harder to tackle. It can be emotionally wrenching to look around and see other teenagers who seem to be doing so well while yours is not. Clients tell me all the time how difficult it is for them to see the teenage child of a neighbor or family member who seems to be perfect in every way when their own child is struggling. All I can say is that, first, you never know what goes on in other people's homes, and second, you can only do your best.

Some teens are hardwired to be strong, self-motivated, and resilient. Those kids are easier to parent because half the work has been done. But children who have tidal-wave emotions, who seem to feel everything more than their peers, need special parenting. Their journey through adolescence is hard for both of you. If you have a teen like this, it is so important to get support. Speak to a professional or reach out to someone in the community. The worst thing you can do is minimize the problem, because then the underlying message you're sending to your teen is that *he* (not his problem) isn't important.

Looking for the Signs

No adolescent is likely to approach you to say, "Hey Mom, you know, I've been secretly cutting myself and I really want to stop" or "Hey Dad, I've been throwing up after every meal and I need your help." If you have any suspicions at all, you need to look for the warning signs.

Cutting

- Unexplained cuts, bruises, or other marks on their body
- Weird excuses for wearing long sleeves in July
- Difficulty expressing emotions (especially if this is a change in behavior)
- More time than usual spent in their room

Anorexia

- Baggy clothes to hide their weight loss
- Dramatic weight loss
- Avoidance of foods they used to eat
- A habit of weighing themselves more than before
- Exercising after eating
- Being fat as a recurring topic of conversation when they're clearly not fat

Bulimia

Bulimia (bingeing and purging) may be more difficult to recognize than anorexia because many bulimics maintain a normal body weight, and may even be overweight. But the toll it takes on the body and the emotional pain it expresses are just as devastating. Here are signs that a teen is bulimic.

- Excessive eating without any weight gain
- An accumulation of food wrappers or packaging in the garbage
- Entering into an almost euphoric or a trance-like state while eating
- Going to the washroom right after meals

Getting Professional Help

The problems we've been talking about here are not the kinds you can take on by yourself. If you know or even suspect that your child is harming herself or has an eating disorder, you need to get professional help. But that doesn't mean you don't have an important role to play.

Although connected parenting in itself can't cure these problems, in combination with other therapies it can help your child deal with the underlying emotional issues, and it may provide the key to making other interventions more effective. Many therapists advise parents to make sure they're close and paying attention to their child, but rarely do they explain how to do that. The assumption seems to be that it's an innate skill all parents have at their disposal, but as you've probably figured out by now, that simply isn't true.

The more you CALM and connect with your teen, the less vulnerable she'll be to seeking out these behaviors in the first place. But that's not to say you should blame yourself or feel guilty if it does happen. There are many elements, some of them genetic, that put a child at greater risk. But again, the closer you are to your teenager the more likely you are to notice the warning signs and thus be able to act on them sooner rather than later.

Could Your Teen Be Suicidal?

No parent wants to believe their child could be so unhappy that he might actually consider ending his life. Nevertheless, according to the Centers for Disease Control, suicide is the third leading cause of death in the United States among adolescents and young adults aged 15 to 24 (following accidents and homicide) and the fourth leading cause of death among children aged 10 to 14. According to the Canadian Mental Health Association, suicide accounts for 24 percent of all deaths among 15- to 24-year-olds and 16 percent of 16- to 44-year-olds. Suicide is the second leading cause of death for Canadians between the ages of 10 and 24. Seventy-three percent of hospital admissions for attempted suicide are for people between the ages of 15 and 44.

The adolescent propensity for suicide may be partly explained by the still-developing frontal lobe we discussed in Chapter One. Teens have extreme reactions to virtually everything, from getting dumped by a boyfriend to not being invited to a party. They lack the ability to step back and take the longer view that would allow them to understand that they aren't going to feel so bad for the rest of their lives. The best thing you as a parent can do after mirroring—without nagging or invalidating their feelings by reminding them, yet again, that you know better than they do—is to gently remind them that this setback doesn't signal the end of the world and that they will feel better, probably sooner than they think.

Since virtually all teens spend a fair amount of time complaining that "life sucks" and announcing "I wish I were never born"—some may even say they wish they were dead—it can be tough to figure out when to take them seriously. But what you can say is, "I know you're saying these things to explain how upset you really are, but if you keep talking about not wanting to be alive and proclaiming that your life is over, I have to take it seriously. So whether you mean it or not, we're going to have to go to the hospital." What generally happens then is that the kids who are simply being dramatic will stop. The danger of ignoring these signs, however, is that the kid who really is in trouble might think to himself, *Jeez, here I am talking about killing myself and they're still not paying attention. What do I have to do to get some attention?* So you run the risk of his escalating the behavior.

Here are the warning signs you really need to pay attention to:

- Radical changes in behavior, such as a generally outgoing teen suddenly becoming withdrawn
- Flatness of affect, meaning that a teen doesn't get particularly excited about anything
- Abuse of drugs or alcohol
- Carelessness about appearance (which doesn't mean that a kid who's always been a slob has a mental health issue)

- A drop in grades or loss of interest in school
- A sudden disregard for authority
- Unexplained headaches or stomachaches
- Aggressive outbursts
- The harming of animals

Teens can sometimes be so odd in the way they present themselves that it's difficult to tell whether they're depressed or just being teenagers. It's better to be safe than sorry, however; so if you're the least bit worried, even though you may think you're overreacting or being crazy, check it out with their doctor, a counselor at school, or, if necessary, the hospital. If you hear your child say anything about killing himself, you need to listen. Always be attentive, especially if he doesn't seem particularly upset when he's saying it. If he walks out of the room, don't leave him alone. And if he lets you know he's been thinking about *how* to kill himself, get him into the car and to the hospital immediately or call 911.

Providing a Safe Haven

We've been talking all along about how much more stressful the world is for today's teens than it was for most of us when we were growing up. That's why, no matter how much they strain against it, teenagers need to feel the tension on the rope you're holding to keep them safe. No matter how well you listen, how much you mirror, and how connected you are to your teen, there's a chance he or she will experience some kind of serious emotional problem. But if you've established a strong connection with your child and if he's comfortable confiding his feelings, the more likely it is that you'll recognize when he's in danger while the problem is still in its early stages.

NINE

Highly Emotional and Exceptional Teens

Every child is precious; every child is unique. Some find life more challenging than others, but there is virtually no child whose life can't be made better by an understanding, nurturing, and empathic relationship with her parents. That said, even if your teen doesn't fall into any of the "exceptional" categories discussed below, this chapter has important information for you.

Dandelions and Orchids: They're Both Flowers

In the journal *Development and Psychopathology*, Bruce Ellis, a psychologist, and W. Thomas Boyce, a pediatrician, point out that the Swedes have long talked about "dandelion" and "orchid" children. The "dandelions" are "normal," "healthy," and genetically "resilient." Like the weeds after which they're named, these children are likely to do well wherever they're "planted"—that is, in any environment. You can ignore them, forget to water them, and they just bounce back. The authors compare these children to those they call "orchids." Orchid children are born with particular genetic variants that make them much more sensitive to virtually any stimulus. We've known for some time that, depending on their environment, people with these genetic differences are more likely than others to become depressed, anxious, or antisocial. But Ellis and Boyce suggest that in the right environment, these same children can also bloom much more spectacularly than any dandelion. In other words, they're like hothouse flowers that will either wither with neglect or mistreatment or grow into dazzling blooms when properly cared for.

Many orchid kids overreact to their environment and are highly sensitive to all negative stimuli, from smells and tastes to textures and tone of voice. These are the kids who are often anxious. They say you're yelling when you're not. They take everything personally. Just as orchids need the right amount of water, light, and warmth to thrive, orchid children are dependent on being raised in a highly nurturing environment. When they're exposed to positive stimuli, they're capable of amazing things and can be happier, more well-rounded, and more resilient than their dandelion counterparts.

Interestingly, long before I read about Ellis and Boyce's theory, I thought of many of the children I work with as delicate flowers. That's how I prefer to look at children who are exceptional in any way.

Different Causes, but Many of the Same Effects

ADHD (attention deficit hyperactivity disorder), nonverbal learning disabilities, and Asperger's syndrome are innate neurological problems that can, to one degree or another, affect a child's ability to understand, interact, and thrive in the world. Although the problems originate in the wiring of the brain, they manifest in behaviors that may seem unexpected or inappropriate. How the world responds to these behaviors causes the brain to continue developing in particular ways, and a kind of vicious circle is established. The trick, therefore, is to develop strategies that help the brain create more positive or effective behaviors that elicit more positive responses and potentially change to some degree the way the brain is wired.

Most exceptional children are anxious to some extent. Anxiety and its effects are their constant companions and often get in the way of happiness and change. In many cases the cycle begins in infancy. If your baby was born with ADHD, for example, when you did that instinctive mirroring, he may have heard your voice and seen your face, but he also saw the pattern the light was making on the ceiling and heard the sound of the curtain rustling. He wasn't completely focused on you and didn't absorb the full force of your mirroring. Then, as time passed and the baby wasn't responding as positively as you expected, you might have mirrored less. But whether you did or didn't, your baby's brain may not have gotten the full force of those reward chemicals that come with limbic bonding. It wasn't your fault, and it's not too late to change that brain chemistry.

People with ADHD tend to be dynamic, funny risk-takers who push boundaries and think outside the box. They are sensitive, kinetic, and often very intelligent. Many choose careers in emergency services, or become athletes or explorers. If your child has been diagnosed with ADHD or a learning disability, you're already aware of the challenges involved, but sometimes as the child matures there are new issues to deal with. Some problems that weren't so acute when he was little become more so when he gets older, while others tend to decline in importance or even resolve themselves entirely. Poor impulse control, often a part of

ADHD, has more frightening implications during adolescence than earlier. Social problems tend to be magnified in the teen years, when interactions become more verbal, but it's also at this age that kids tend to find and gravitate toward others who are more like themselves. Many find a group they can fit into.

Teens with ADHD are often accused of not listening or paying attention when the real problem is that they're listening and paying attention to everything at once, which means that it's very difficult, if not impossible, to focus on one thing. For these kids life is like standing in the middle of the midway at an amusement park. Someone is yelling "Hot dogs, hot dogs!" while someone else is screaming for you to spin the wheel and win a prize, lights are flashing all around, and the smell of buttered popcorn is mingling with the smell of burgers and cotton candy. Kids with ADHD are living in this kind of carnival atmosphere all the time. And so even though they're often very bright, they tend to miss many of the signals, both subtle and not so subtle, that would help them respond appropriately. As a result, it's not unusual for ADHD teens to be two or three years behind their peers socially and emotionally.

Children with nonverbal learning disabilities have many of the same problems as those with ADHD, but for different reasons. They're often intelligent and articulate but lack some of the neurological wiring that would allow them to "read" nonverbal cues, which can and does put them at a distinct disadvantage in social situations.

Finally, with Asperger's Disorder, there are also neurological anomalies, not yet specifically defined, that prevent people from intuitively grasping or comprehending the nuances of social discourse that seem to come naturally to most of us.

While connected parenting cannot "cure" these disorders, there are many techniques parents can use to make their lives easier and more rewarding.

ADHD: Mental Overload

Our image of the little kid with ADHD is probably a child who can't sit still, who's zooming around the room like a whirling dervish and being generally disruptive. That's a stereotype, but it's also accurate, at least to some degree.

It's tough enough for parents, and people in general, to cope with ADHD when children are small, but the older they get the more we expect them to be able to "just sit still and pay attention." They can learn to get better at it, but it isn't easy—and in some ways it gets harder.

By the time kids are in high school, most classes are conducted in lecture format. More or less by definition, this means they have to stay alert, focused, and still for long periods of time. They have to listen to one voice—the teacher's—while filtering out all the other sounds and distractions that are constantly assaulting them. They feel a disconnect with the material and are exhausted from sitting all day listening to boring stuff. That effort is extremely fatiguing for children with ADHD. As a result, they're more likely than most to zone out, bug peers, or go into that time warp or fugue state discussed in Chapter Six, no matter how determined they are not to. And they're likely to have the same difficulty sticking to curfews and making appointments punctually. They tend to procrastinate, lose track of time, and find it hard to plan, organize, and follow through on a given task.

Of course, at some level these problems aren't very different from those experienced by many adolescents, but in kids with ADHD they're exaggerated and more difficult to overcome.

You can help them by first using the CALM technique and empathizing and then presenting the problem. Let's say you've received a call from your son's teacher saying that he didn't bring his book to school. The teacher's complaint might have gone something like this: "You know, this is the third day in a row your son didn't have his book. We dumped out his backpack and I couldn't believe the mess he had in there. He just isn't trying." This kind of forgetfulness wouldn't be unusual for a kid with ADHD, and it can be frustrating for their teachers who know that the kids are smart enough but not reaching their potential. Unlike a physical disability, ADHD is invisible, so what teachers see is the intelligence, not the disability. As a result, even though they should know better, they chalk it up to laziness or lack of effort.

So how do you handle the situation? Your instinctive reaction may be to echo his teacher's anger and frustration. The minute the kid (we'll call him Morgan) walks through the door, you might say, "Sit, down. We need to talk." Morgan immediately shuts down while you're still revving up. "I got another call from your teacher today. This is ridiculous. When are you going to start figuring out …?" and out comes a laundry list of his errors and omissions stored up over the previous weeks or even months. Morgan, however, has stopped listening. His heart is pounding. Cortisol is rushing to his bloodstream. He feels like a failure who's let his parents down yet again. What he's likely to say is "You're always all over me. You're always bugging me. You don't even know what goes on in school …" and your response will be "How can you say that? We've had this conversation at least fifty times. How many times do I have to say …" And eventually one or the other of you storms out of the room. You've probably had this conversation fifty *thousand* times, and you'll have it another fifty thousand times, because in that dialogue there's not one ounce of motivation for Morgan to change. It's not so much what you say in these conversations as how you make your child feel. If he walks away feeling bad about himself, feeling that he can't do anything right and that you don't love him, then he won't have been given the support and guidance he needs to change.

Here's a different scenario using the CALM technique. Morgan walks through the door and you say, "Hi. So how are you doing?" Just from that greeting, he'll probably know something is up. You see the look in his eyes, so you say, "Here's the deal. I just got a call from your teacher, and before you say anything, I want you to know that I'm going to try for once not to say too much, because I know I do that all the time." By saying this you're preempting Morgan's probable initial reaction. Then you continue, "I don't want to have the same conversation we've always had. I want to try to help you. I want to see if this conversation can go differently. It has to be exhausting for you to hear the same thing over and over again and feel as though I'm not on your side."

Morgan may not believe you. He might even say something like, "Oh yeah, I've heard that before. You'll be yelling at me in five minutes anyway." To which you might reply, "You *have* heard it from me before. I'm honestly trying to figure out what's going on here, because in your mind you've got everything under control. It's kind of working for you, and if it's not, you think it's the best you can do. And then there's your teacher, who thinks it's a problem ..." You'll need to make two or three statements like that. And Morgan might respond, "Well, I do have it under control. You never trust me." To which you might reply, "When I think about that, when I hear you say that, I can't imagine how that makes you feel, to constantly think that your parents don't trust you, and given how many times we've had these conversations, I get why you feel that way." And Morgan says, "Yeah, well, welcome to my life." You can register that again by saying, "It doesn't seem fair that as soon as you see me or any adult coming, you think, Here we go *again!*"

After three or four of those CALM statements, you present the problem. "I really do want this conversation to go differently, and I want you to have the skills you need to get where you need to go."

Sometimes you need to be brave enough to just end it there and say, "Let's both go away and think about what we can do differently, how we can help each other with this." If your teen has some understanding of her ADHD, you could say, "You know, your ADHD is getting in the way. It's taking away positive things that could happen for you. But we can outsmart it. We can figure out a way to use the part of your brain that is very smart. We can compensate. We can strategize. But let's not go down the same road we've always gone. Let's both think about it."

Some teens might actually do that, but most will just go back to their room and play a video game. Even so, they will have received the message. They will have lodged somewhere in the back of their mind the thought, "Well, that went differently." We tend to think we have to solve every problem immediately, but sometimes it takes a few conversations. In this situation your next dialogue might be along these lines: "So, okay, have you thought about it?" To which Morgan will probably just grunt. So you say, "Okay, I'm not going to push you, but I've been thinking, and this is what I've come up with ..." That could be the opening to a conversation about the ADHD brain. You might say, "You're very capable. You're good at ..." And you can cite all the things you know he's good at. "But your brain struggles with organizing it all and dealing with the stuff you think is boring ..." ADHD kids *hate* being bored. It's as if they were allergic to boredom. And then you might conclude the conversation by suggesting that he try dealing with the problem of left-behind books himself.

Give him two weeks to show you that he can handle it. If he does, great. If not, at the end of that time you say, "It really sucks, thinking you can make it work and then it doesn't work the way you thought it would. But that just means we need to try something different. We have to wake up the part of your brain that tends to fall asleep. The more you use the part of your brain that organizes

and supervises, the stronger it will be. It's kind of like working out."
And then you lay out your plan. "You know, I love you enough for
you to be mad at me about this, but here's what we're putting into
place ..." At which point you need to let him know what's expected
and what the consequence will be if he can't live up to that expectation. It may also be helpful to introduce the concept of the now
self and future self that we discussed earlier. Then follow up with a
message of competence, such as "I believe you can do this."

Having these conversations and implementing these strategies
take time. You need to be patient enough to go through it all over
and over again. And you need to take your cue from your teen.
When you see he's stopped listening, it's time to shut up. All kids—
but ADHD kids in particular—have a limited attention span. Our
instinctive reaction when a kid is shutting us out is to start talking
louder and longer, but that doesn't work—especially with ADHD
kids. When they turn us off it's not because they're being defiant,
it's because there are so many things happening when you're
talking—your words, your tone of voice, your facial expressions,
and so on—that it's too much for their brains to process. You have
to deliver your message in short, powerful packets so that they can
walk away and let what you've said sink in.

Many parents find these conversations difficult. After all, we've
already learned the lessons about the importance of punctuality and
paying attention, and we don't want our kids to have to learn them
the hard way. But kids rarely learn by being lectured to. Most need
to experience real consequences before the information is stored
properly in their brains. That parental rope needs to be slack
enough for them to feel the fall but tight enough to prevent them
from getting seriously hurt.

It's also important that you present the problem in a way that's
relevant to them; otherwise, they won't buy into it. It has to be
about making *their* life better, not about what *you* need or want

from them. Since kids are so into technology, why not use what's available to help them? There are high-tech watches and cellphones with built-in alarms. Most smart phones have an application that allows you to create a checklist of tasks and deadlines.

There is no perfect way to know how much to advocate for your teen, how much to intervene, and when to just let them experience the consequences of their actions. The issue can be particularly difficult when you're dealing with a special needs kid. On the school front, you can try to enlist the aid of the guidance counselor to help your teen choose the courses most likely to engage his interest. It might also be a good idea to speak to the principal or another appropriate administrator and explain that your child has ADHD and may need to get up and walk around for a minute during class. Sometimes he or she will cooperate and sometimes not, but you can try.

You can also help your child improve her skills at teacher management. Teachers are human, grades are subjective, and sometimes a kid's reputation precedes her as she moves from one grade to the next. But you can help your child change the way she's perceived by helping her master a few simple strategies. Most teachers look with favor on kids who appear to be alert, attentive, and responsive. Suggest that your child pay attention to what the "good" kids—the ones the teacher favors—are doing in class and try to emulate them. It may be as simple as looking the teacher in the eye, nodding from time to time, or saying good morning when he enters the room. You're not asking her to be a phony or to become someone she isn't; you're just helping her become aware of those behavioral signals she may have missed because of her ADHD.

And because ADHD is related to impulse control, these are the kids who are most likely to engage in risky behaviors, meaning that—even more than most teens—they're likely to act first and think later (or not at all). They don't stop and say to themselves, *Hey, the last time I did this it didn't work out so well. Maybe I shouldn't do it again.* They're also the ones who tend to get "caught" when they're just doing what the rest of the kids are doing. Because they're so constantly distracted, they may not spot the authority figure approaching or notice that their friends have suddenly gone quiet or slipped away. And when they are confronted, they may not know what they did to get into trouble. After a while they begin to assume they're going to be in trouble no matter what they do. The cortisol is already pumping in their brain each time they walk into a social situation. They may start acting the part of the class clown when they have missed concepts or don't understand. Most kids would rather look bad than unintelligent. They may start withdrawing and isolating themselves, or self-medicating with street drugs.

Often kids like this also self-medicate by engaging in risky or inappropriate behaviors that generate an adrenaline rush. They need that hormonal rush to stimulate the frontal lobe so that it can do its job, which is to suppress impulsive behaviors. It's a paradoxical effect, but it's the same effect that occurs when a kid with ADHD takes a medication like Ritalin or Adderall, both of which are stimulants. If a child who didn't have ADHD, or an adult for that matter, took one of these drugs, they'd be flying off the wall in all directions. But for those with ADHD the drug has the opposite effect: it stimulates their normally understimulated frontal lobe, brings the brain into balance, and allows them to think and focus.

Parents are often reluctant to put their kids on prescription medications because they worry about potential side effects, which might include loss of appetite or difficulty sleeping and which the prescribing physician will have taken into account and discussed with the patient and his parents. But the social and psychological downsides of not taking appropriate medication can be worse than any medical side effects. Sometimes medication acts as a kind of life preserver: if someone is drowning, there's no point in standing on the shore and yelling out instructions on how to swim. The drowning person won't hear you. If they're wearing a life preserver, however, they can begin to benefit from the lessons you have to teach.

Often, of course, teens being teens, they resist taking the medication they've been prescribed precisely when they need it most to help them focus better on their schoolwork. I often tell parents to let their kids try going without their meds so that they can see the results for themselves. Sometimes they need proof that the meds are really helping them. If possible, choose a time when it will have the least effect on your teen's grades. Agree on a period of time: tell her, for example, that you'll go along with the experiment for a month. But make it clear that if she starts to miss curfews, if her schoolwork suffers, or if other unwanted behaviors are reappearing, it's important to go back on the meds. Don't nag during the time you've agreed on, and if it doesn't work out, *don't* say "I told you so." When the time is up, and if it's clear that the medication is necessary, mirror to let her know you appreciate how she's feeling. Because you gave her the opportunity to, in effect, control her own destiny, she's more likely to see the benefits and comply (although she might still complain).

Nonverbal LDs: When the "Receiver" Doesn't Work So Well

A nonverbal learning disability is particularly hard on a child when he reaches adolescence and social interactions are so much more frequent and complicated. While kids with ADHD generally understand on some level that they're "screwing things up," kids with a nonverbal LD may not even realize they're doing something wrong. They just keep walking head-on into the same situation and getting picked on or laughed at. They're painfully aware that things aren't going well, but they don't know how to fix them. This can be heartbreaking for a parent, or any caring person, to watch.

Although they generally excel at verbal skills, they tend to deliver long monologues and don't "see" the facial expressions that would let them know that their audience has lost interest or that their jokes are falling flat. They may stand too close or talk too loud. They may not notice that even though they're wearing the same jeans as the cool kids, they've got them hitched up too high. They can be clumsy. They may be poor at sports or video games because their hand–eye coordination is undeveloped. What makes matters worse is that by adolescence most interactions between kids are based on banter, storytelling, and the sharing of thoughts, opinions, and ideas. The rapid pace and rhythm of these conversations is likely to be too much for teens with nonverbal LDs, leaving them lonely and isolated.

And kids with a nonverbal LD—particularly adolescent girls—may be at greater risk of sexual exploitation. Because they don't intuitively understand body language, they're often unaware of the signals their own physical presentation is sending. They may sit with their legs apart or not notice that their shirt is hiked up or unbuttoned. Or they just don't "get" the significance of these things. And then, when someone responds to these unintentional signals, they don't realize that they may be in danger. It's not that they can't learn to present themselves more appropriately, but they need to be coached. Parents of these kids have a heightened responsibility to keep them safe.

One technique I've found to work is to have your teen sit in front of a mirror and show her what it looks like when she's sitting in a short skirt. Begin, as always, by mirroring: "You know, it's so funny that we have all these rules about how to sit and what parts of our body it's okay to show. You just want to be comfortable, and I get that. Little kids don't have to worry about these things, and it's sad that when you get older things start to change." Then introduce your agenda: "I love you and I want you to be comfortable with your body. I don't want you to be self-conscious, but here's the thing. If you sit like that, someone could make fun of you or want to touch you in a way that makes you uncomfortable." Then use the mirror to demonstrate what you mean. She might "get it" visually when she wouldn't if you simply explained the concept. You might also consider agreeing on a subtle, nonverbal signal, which you practise and no one else would recognize, to use as a reminder when you see her sitting that way.

It can be a difficult topic, and you need to approach it with the right balance: to be serious without being heavy-handed. Kids at this age are generally not comfortable in their own bodies anyway, and you don't want to make them even more self-conscious than they already are. But, as always, mirroring and connecting can make it easier to present and resolve the problem.

Kids don't generally help other kids to figure out what they're doing wrong; they just roll their eyes or walk away, or make some disparaging remark, such as "Oh my god, you're so annoying." This kind of rejection leaves the LD kid feeling hurt and bewildered because he's trying so hard and never seems to get it right. It's difficult and painful for parents, too, who find themselves watching helplessly while their child endures this treatment day after day. But these kids are very intelligent, and you *can* help them. There's a lot you can do.

Parents are often the only ones who give their LD children accurate feedback. First mirror and let them know you understand and empathize, and then discuss the problem with them. The more they understand their strengths and weaknesses, the better able they'll be to use the former to get around the latter.

With kids who have nonverbal LDs, you may need to be very concrete, giving specific examples, not just general concepts. You might, for example, explain that their brain is especially good at processing facts, which is why they love to talk about things they know, but it doesn't manage pictures and patterns as easily. "When people talk to one another they make pictures with their expressions and patterns with their language. Your brain tends not to get the messages they're sending. It's not that your brain can't understand these things; it's just that it would rather focus on hard information. So you need to exercise your brain so that you start to make new connections. When you talk to someone there are things you can look for that tell you how he's reacting. If he turns his eyes away or if he says 'Yeah, yeah, I get it,' you'll know you're talking too much. I know these things might not seem important to you, but they're important to other people, and that might be why kids sometimes don't want to spend time with you or invite you to their house. Maybe your good friends don't care, but a lot of other people do."

Kids with nonverbal LDs tend sometimes to be loud and to talk and joke around too much. ADHD and even gifted kids (who may become so exuberant and involved in what they're saying that they don't pay attention to how other people are reacting) can do this too. I often suggest they adopt what I call the 50 percent rule. If they just tone down their delivery by 50 percent, they'll probably be right on pitch.

Sometimes there's a precipitating event you can use as a jumping-off point. One of my clients, for example, had been friendly with a popular group of kids, but found that when she returned to school after vacation they'd suddenly shut her out. She was devastated. When she talked to me about it I first mirrored how terrible she felt and then went on to figure out what had happened and what she could do to prevent it from happening again. She liked the idea of the 50 percent rule. She felt it was actually empowering because it gave her a plan and helped her feel more in control. As always, it's important first to mirror and empathize before you offer this solution. If you don't, your teen will simply feel criticized and invalidated.

You can also use family situations to provide concrete examples of socially inappropriate behavior. Maybe you could say something like "You know, we love you, and even we were getting annoyed at dinner last night when you didn't give anyone else a chance to talk. We love it that you know so many interesting things, but it's important to let other people express themselves too. Otherwise it's a monologue, not a conversation. The greatest comics in the world know how to time themselves so that their monologue doesn't go on too long." Just make sure when you're doing this that you remain neutral and mindful of their embarrassment. And be sure to sound like you're in their corner and not siding with others.

In essence, most of the time your teen has missed the connection between cause and effect. So, you need to approach the problem as if you were a social psychologist. You need to help him see how his behavior contributed to the outcome, whether it was an insult or ostracism, and figure out what he can do to make things go differently in the future. As a teaching tool, you can also use the reality television viewing technique discussed in Chapter Seven. The point is to do what you can to help him fit in.

Sometimes parents are so proud of their kid's knowledge and verbal skills that they too may not see the effect he has on others. I'm not saying parents shouldn't be proud, or that they should discourage their kids from using what they're good at, but if they spend too much time praising their children's verbal accomplishments they may encourage behavior that isn't going to help them in the teen world they inhabit.

One of the kindest (and easiest) things you can do to help your child fit in is to buy him the coolest clothes you can afford. I know this sounds shallow, and you certainly don't want to convey the message that the worth of an individual depends on the clothes he wears. But if a teen is having trouble fitting in with his peers, going to school wearing shoes with Velcro closures isn't going to help matters. The point is that kids with nonverbal LDs don't see the details that make a particular piece of clothing either cool or dorky. So he might, for example, see a popular boy wearing a pair of jeans and think, *Okay, he's wearing jeans, so jeans are cool*. But he wouldn't see that his own jeans are too short, baggy, or high-waisted. You need to take him to the coolest store (and if you don't know what that is, ask another teenager), go up to the coolest-looking salesperson, and just say, "Can you help my son with the latest trends?" Like it or not, clothing matters—to adults as well as kids—and you don't want to make things harder for him than they already are.

The good news for these kids is that when they graduate from middle school, things often become easier. Since high schools tend to be bigger, it gets easier for them to find other kids with whom they fit in. Meanwhile, make sure they participate in the kinds of activities at which they can be successful and meet peers with similar interests. It's also okay to encourage them to hang out with cousins or family friends. If a kid has just one good friend, he or she will be okay.

Asperger's Disorder: Finding Their Niche

Kids with Asperger's Disorder have many of the same issues as those with nonverbal LDs, but with a major difference: most—but certainly not all—Asperger's children won't notice that they're being excluded and often won't really care. The blessing (if you can call it that) is that *because* they don't care they're less likely than LD kids to become the target of teasing.

Many children with Asperger's struggle with etiquette, standard social greetings, and the pragmatics of language. They don't see why they should say "Hi, how are you?" when they see someone they know, because often they don't care how they are or don't care if anyone neglects to say hi to them. But they *can* learn that a greeting is expected and that they need to do it. And as they practice, the positive responses they get will act as reinforcement for the behavior. It may never be second nature, but these social customs can be learned.

Interestingly, society seems to have adapted more and more to the Asperger's brain in recent years. Some people in the mental health community believe that the so-called nerds of the world really fall somewhere on the Asperger's spectrum, but since computer techies and geeks, for example, have gained so much respect they're no longer considered odd, much less disabled. A kid can now be totally isolated, sitting in front of his computer, and have friends all over the world. They may not meet one another at Starbucks for a latte, and their friendships may not resemble what we consider a social relationship, but they "talk" about things that are relevant to them, and are friends.

Like kids with nonverbal LDs, Asperger's kids seem to find their niche as they get older. Their world expands, they find other kids like themselves to hang out with, and their "oddity" becomes less apparent.

Many parents have asked me whether mirroring works with an Asperger's kid or whether he just won't get it. I tell them they should mirror *even more* with these kids than they would with others. I've had great success with Asperger's kids in my practice. I remember one mother in particular who said, "I can't believe it! His sister fell and my son actually bent down and asked, 'Are you all right?'" Mirroring isn't a miracle cure, but it feels good, it bypasses language and releases endorphins in the brain, and it will help your child reach his full potential.

By mirroring, you help Asperger's kids get more comfortable with surprises. They want structure and predictability; they hate anything unexpected and become very anxious when their world becomes disordered. Most of us find this aversion difficult to understand, because most of us love the surprises and breaks in routine that upset them. A day like Ferris Bueller's day off (in the film of the same name) would flip them out completely. But you can't impose your version of "happy" on your kids.

You can, though, work with your teen by warning him of imminent disruptions: "We're going to throw something into our schedule today that we haven't planned. We're going to stop for lunch on the way home." Or it might be stopping at the dry cleaners, getting a haircut, or picking up something at the drugstore. Once you've delivered the message, mirror to let him know that you understand he may be feeling a bit anxious about this but that you know he's going to be okay. You want to help him become more comfortable with change, because no one can be in control of every aspect of their life, and the older a child gets, the truer that becomes.

It can, of course, be something of a balancing act: how much do you protect your child and how much do you push him? It will be different for every child. If you only protect, he'll be in even bigger trouble later in life, but if you push too much he may become paralyzed with fear and anxiety. Using the CALM technique and frontloading while explaining to your teen what the plan is and predicting what's likely to happen will be a highly effective addition to whatever you're already doing.

Dysnomia: The Other End of the Spectrum

Dysnomia, which is characterized by an inability to retrieve words from memory, is at the other end of the spectrum from nonverbal LDs. In order to express herself, the child with dysnomia has to search through the memory bank in her brain. That takes time and effort. Normally we speak without thinking much about where the words are coming from; it's what's called an associative task. But when we have to think about each word before speaking, it becomes a cognitive task.

Kids with dysnomia, or any expressive or receptive vocabulary issue, probably don't talk very much, because it's hard work for them. And when they do try to have a conversation, instead of maintaining eye contact they're apt to look up or stare off into the distance as they search for the next word. Like kids with nonverbal LDs, but for a different reason, they miss the facial expressions and other social cues that most of us take for granted. They tend to get into trouble because they can't easily explain themselves or charm people into forgiving them. And, for the same reasons, they're at greater risk of being misunderstood and left out.

If you're the parent of a child who struggles with language, asking her to tell you "what's wrong" or "what happened" when she's upset is only going to compound the problem. She finds it difficult to express herself at the best of times, but when she's upset she's not going to be able to search through all those words filed away in her brain in order to come up with an answer. Instead of quizzing her, first mirror and then say, "What do I need to know? Think about what's important for me to know about what happened. I'm going to leave you to do that and I'll be back in a few minutes." If you step away, and give her the time to think about what she wants to say, she'll be able to tell you.

Disabilities Are Relative

Learning disabilities are defined by their relevance to society. If you lived in a world where all conversation was sung, and your ability to converse was judged on how well you carried a tune, tone deafness would be a disability. And because the ability to carry a tune—like the ability to read facial expressions or to retrieve words from memory—is hardwired in the brain, no matter how hard you tried you could never become a brilliant singer. You could take lessons, and perhaps become a better singer, but you'd still be at a disadvantage. The same is true for kids with any kind of learning disability. They need support, advocacy, and to feel that home is a place where they're loved and cherished. Knowing that will give them the strength and resilience they need to face the outside world. Incidental and conversational mirroring is critically important for these teens. They can, with love and support, learn to compensate and to advocate for themselves, but they'll always have a more difficult time than kids who don't have their disability.

Anxiety Can Also Be Disabling

Many adolescents become anxious at one time or another—it goes along with the developmental changes they're experiencing. To them, the success or failure of every social interaction may appear to have life or death consequences. At the same time, they're under a lot of pressure to earn high marks and get into a good college. They're in the process of pulling away from you and figuring out who they are. They realize that their childhood is almost over and may be wondering how that happened so fast. They swing back and forth between wanting to be a kid again and wanting to be an adult. Because their frontal lobe isn't fully developed, they have a hard time acquiring a sense of perspective on their life. Meanwhile, they're hanging around with a bunch of other people who can't help them out because they're all in the same boat. As a result of all this, teens can easily become overwhelmed. Your teenage daughter may not want to leave the house because she's having a bad hair day. Your adolescent son might disappear into his room with his computer. For most kids, those "off" days aren't the norm. But for some, the anxiety can become so generalized that it leads to disabling panic attacks.

Many people with anxiety become afraid of being afraid, and that terrible cycle of self-perpetuating fearfulness can make their lives difficult. Typically, the anxious person records the events that triggered a panic attack in the part of her brain that stores emotional memories. Then, when she anticipates encountering a similar situation, the memory is revived: it triggers the same emotions, and sends her into fight-or-flight mode. Panic may be felt as a physical sensation—most often as a headache, stomachache, tightness in the chest, or difficulty breathing.

Polly, for example, became a patient of mine when, at the age of sixteen, she started to have panic attacks every time she went to the mall. Rationally, she knew her anxiety made no sense, but there was nothing she could do about it. She'd get chest pains, hyperventilate, and feel as if she were about to throw up. The problem became more acute until it developed into generalized social anxiety. If Polly arrived at school to see a group of kids already talking to one another, she'd become anxious, worrying that she wouldn't be able to join the conversation or that they'd ignore her. Eventually her anxiety got so bad that she refused to go out with her friends and saw them only when they came to her house. She'd go to the mall with her mother, but she wouldn't let her out of her sight.

We treated her anxiety using a behavior modification technique. As a first step, I told Polly to go to the mall and let her mother walk around the corner for one minute. She could time it on her watch, and after one minute her mother would come back. I also told her mom that she shouldn't make a big deal of these comings and goings. It's important *not* to make your teen feel as if she's done something remarkable: that would only make her even more anxious. Each week we upped the ante by extending the time her mother was out of sight until Polly was comfortable for an extended period on her own. Eventually, she didn't need her mom and could go to the mall with a friend.

In Polly's case there was no obvious reason for the initial onset of anxiety, but in other cases, particularly if a child has never before been particularly anxious, there may be a triggering event. That was the case with Melanie, a popular girl who interacted easily with other kids until she got a part in a school play that another girl had coveted. The other girl sent nasty text messages about Melanie to her friends at school. She persuaded them to turn away and snub Melanie whenever Melanie tried to join the group, and basically shut her out of all their activities.

Melanie had never been on the receiving end of this kind of behavior before, and it hit her hard. It was also devastating for her parents. Many of us tend, at least in some small way, to believe that if our child is being bullied or ostracized she must be doing something to cause the behavior. But even the most popular kid in the world can be the victim of this kind of rejection. Melanie's first panic attack came without warning when she was watching *American Idol* with her mother at home. She was apparently perfectly relaxed when suddenly she felt as if she couldn't breathe.

I advised Melanie's parents to pull up the safety net for a while, and perhaps let her sleep on the sofa or a mattress on the floor of their bedroom if that helped relax her, but also to let her know that the arrangement was temporary and that she'd go back to her own bed when she felt ready. In addition I emphasized how important it was that they use the CALM technique not only when she was upset but as often as possible throughout the course of the day. Conversational mirroring and the connecting play we discussed in

Chapter Three are essential for helping anxious kids. Remember that oxytocin blocks cortisol, the stress hormone, so lots of love and oxytocin are the best antidotes to anxiety. Stay with it to help your teen strengthen and rebuild. Like the element on an electric stove that takes awhile to cool down, anxiety lingers as a protective response, and until that element cools down, many things are going to make an anxious teen nervous and reactive.

Finally, I cautioned Melanie's parents that, whatever else they did, they needed to take seriously what Melanie was feeling and to avoid saying things like "C'mon, you're not a baby so stop acting like one." It took several months. Melanie did have a couple more panic attacks, but gradually her anxiety diminished and the attacks disappeared completely.

If panic attacks aren't addressed, after a while you begin to panic because you're afraid you're going to panic. Think of anxiety as a campfire: the more anxious you get, the more logs you throw on the fire. If you're in a situation where you aren't particularly anxious, the flames may appear to go out but the embers are still burning. All it takes is a tiny bit of fuel, maybe just a single comment or incident, for the fire to flare up again.

This is actually a biochemical response. If your brain perceives danger, your body prepares to respond to the imminent attack by releasing adrenaline and the stress hormone cortisol. Both mentally and physically you're on high alert, and it takes some time to calm yourself from the inside out so that both your brain and your body chemistry can return to normal.

When someone is in the throes of an anxiety attack, no amount of logic is going to talk him out of it. Because his frontal lobe isn't working, we're trying to reason with his primitive reptilian impulses. Ridiculous as this may sound, imagine for a moment that you're standing on a 300-foot-high bridge and someone is trying to persuade you to jump. He gives you all kinds of rational reasons to believe that jumping is perfectly safe. He quotes statistics and shows you videos of people who have jumped off the same bridge and not been hurt. It won't matter because everything in your brain is telling you that if you jump you're going to die, and you'll continue to do everything in your power to send the message to the other person that jumping really, truly is dangerous. That's just how your teen feels when he's anxious. To him, in that moment, you might as well be saying that it's perfectly safe to jump off a 300-foot-high bridge, and until you let him know that you understand what he's trying to tell you about his fear and anxiety, he won't be able to hear anything you have to say.

It's not uncommon for anxious kids to have this kind of fear about going to school. Overcoming the child's resistance and getting him to deal with his fears can seem impossible. The stress caused by the daily struggle can leave parents swinging between anger at their child's defiance and terror that he'll fall into a pattern of avoiding unpleasant or difficult situations for the rest of his life. Your first task—and it can be a difficult one—is to figure out whether his action has a behavioral cause, meaning that the choice is still under his control, or is genuine panic, meaning that he has no access to rational thought and no element of choice is involved at all. Once again, mirroring as much as possible, not only about school but also about unrelated issues—both the good things and the bad—tightens that rope, helps build resilience, and encourages risk-taking.

It's very important that your teen not get in the habit of staying home. His decision not to go to school is based on the fight-or-flight mechanism that's telling him to retreat and hide until whatever is frightening him goes away. School, however, does not go away, and the longer he hides, the more unmanageable the problem becomes. So even if you have to sit in the car or in the school office all day just to be available, it's better than letting him stay home.

But whether it's fear of going to school or some other issue that's causing the anxiety, by mirroring and making him feel safe enough to confide in you, you'll be able to find out what's bothering him so that you can then work together to come up with a solution. If he's struggling, and his anxiety is getting in the way of his normal activities, it would be wise to consult with his pediatrician or a therapist.

In some cases, if things are really bad, it might be appropriate to change schools or look at some alternative form of schooling. It's a difficult choice and always a judgment call. If his current school is clearly an unsafe emotional environment for him, if he's being bullied or abused by other students or a teacher and the school is doing nothing to improve the situation, removing him from the school might be your only option. But if that's the case, you also need to make sure your child has the tools, and the professional support if necessary, to prevent the problem from following him.

The Drama of the Gifted Child

Children who have an underlying neurological problem are, not surprisingly, more at risk than most of those experiencing increased anxiety, but gifted kids are also susceptible. Being gifted is a blessing, but sometimes it doesn't feel that way.

Unlike most teens, who live in the moment and find it difficult to envision the future, gifted kids tend to see all the potential consequences of the actions they're contemplating (I call them "horizon thinkers"), and that leads them to worry more than most. *If I do this, then that might happen, and then if that happens, this might happen ...* and so on. They're more prone to developing anticipatory anxiety, worrying about events that are years away: *What if I don't marry a good person? What if I don't get a good job? What if I die? What happens when I die?*

Because these kids live so much inside their own head they may fail to pick up the social signals others are sending, not unlike kids with nonverbal learning disabilities. Or they may not understand why it's necessary to engage in such conventional niceties. With a tin ear for context, they may speak to a teacher in the same tone they use when addressing a parent or a friend. They may be bossy, brag a lot, or simply become impatient with kids who aren't as quick or clever as they are. They don't always grasp the "art" of conversation and may find ordinary teen talk uninteresting. To make matters worse, they may find what they're saying so brilliant or amusing that they can't imagine someone else not being as enthralled as they are. They tend to use pretentious vocabulary that alienates them from their peers. And because some gifted kids think about the world in scientific or mathematical terms, they become frustrated with anyone whose behavior seems to them silly or irrational—which would be most of their peers.

They do, however, still want to have friends. When they realize that whatever they're doing in social encounters isn't working, they don't know how to fix it, and so they may withdraw and drop out of the conversation entirely. I often suggest to my gifted clients that they watch some of the television programs other kids are watching: to take some time off from PBS and the History Channel to watch popular teen shows. Then they'll at least have a point of entry into the conversation that their peers can relate to. It's not that they don't understand social skills; it's just that they sometimes don't find these skills relevant to their own situation and so choose not to use them.

As well, because schoolwork is easy for them, they may have trouble getting motivated to study and, therefore, underachieve. Or they may excel in areas that interest them and simply quit if they're bored. And if or when a gifted child discovers something really is difficult for him, he often doesn't know how to handle it. When a kid who's never received a grade below an A– suddenly gets a B on a test, he may perceive that as failure, the end of the world. Since his whole identity has been tied up with being the "smart kid," in order to avoid another failure, he may give up instead of trying harder. Gifted kids often can't conceive of being less than perfect. Fear of failure can make them even more anxious than kids who've had more experience dealing with setbacks.

Finally, a gifted kid who has coasted through high school is more likely to crash when he gets to college, because he hasn't developed any study skills and he hasn't learned to organize his time. A study conducted by Philip Shaw, Judith Rapoport, Jay Giedd, and colleagues at the National Institute of Mental Health and McGill University and reported in the March 30, 2006, issue of *Nature* found that "Magnetic resonance imaging (MRI) scans on [gifted kids] showed that their brain's outer mantle, or cortex, thickens more rapidly during childhood, reaching its peak later than in their peers—perhaps reflecting a longer developmental window for high-level thinking circuitry. It also thins faster during the late teens, likely due to the withering of unused neural connections as the brain streamlines its operations." And according to the NIMH, this effect was particularly true for the prefrontal cortex, which is responsible for executive functions such as planning and organizing.

This may explain why gifted kids have difficulty self-regulating, and why the kid who can do complex math in his head can't find his notebook and arrives to take his final exam without a pen or pencil.

Physiotherapy for the Brain

If one part of the brain is stronger than another, you'll naturally gravitate toward the part that works best. It stands to reason: we all like doing what we're good at. But the brain is an efficient organ; it tends to discard what doesn't get used.

You can help your child use those parts of the brain that he may not be so interested in exercising. Try to sit down with him and explain where he excels and where he needs to practice. A teen may not actually be *below* average in any area, but because one area is so much stronger than the rest, he chooses not to use those parts that are just average. The gap between his strengths and relative weaknesses creates an imbalance, and, as the weaker areas are left unexplored, that gap can widen over time.

Practicing actually builds new neuropathways. There may be parts of the brain your child will never *choose* to use, but with your help, he can learn to strengthen those parts in the same way that he would exercise particular muscle groups to make them stronger. It can be empowering for a kid to know that he can change himself, that he can actually outsmart his brain. This isn't a cure, but rather a way to keep that gap from widening.

Finding the Balance

How do you talk to your teen about his or her challenges or relative weaknesses without making him feel bad about himself? Perhaps more than in any other situation, this is where your mirroring and connecting make all the difference. If your teen is connected to you, he'll know that what you're saying comes from a place of love. And if you're listening and paying attention, you'll know when he's had enough. If he begins to look crestfallen or starts to become defensive, it's time to stop and repair. You can always return to the conversation at a later time.

Exceptional children pose particular challenges for their parents, not least because the traits that make them exceptional are invisible. It can be easy to forget the things that set them apart. Different strategies are called for in each case, but the CALM technique is the starting point for them all.

TEN

Connected Teens FAQs

There are certain questions that come up again and again in my seminars and workshops as well as among my private clients. Even though we've touched on these throughout this book, here's a quick reference guide to common issues.

Won't all the mirroring I do just make my kid more dependent on that kind of support, so that he starts looking for it from other people? Won't it turn him into a wimp?
Exactly the opposite is true. The more you mirror, the less your child will need other people to mirror, because you're building his resilience and independence. You're equipping him with emotional armor, so that when he goes to sports practice and the coach yells at him he'll just think, *Wow, what's with him?* He'll be able to shrug it off instead of feeling injured. And if something upsetting occurs, if he's not invited to a party, for example, he may be hurt and feel bad about it, but he'll be able to let it go and move on. Mirroring strengthens the foundation so that the "house" can withstand even the stormiest weather.

Won't all that empathizing just make her think it's okay to be rude?
No! Except for the incidental mirroring you do in odd moments, there's always a corrective component that follows the mirroring. It's the mirroring that allows your teen to "hear" and respond positively to your guidance. If you skip the mirroring and yell or try to shame her into changing her behavior, chances are she'll walk away thinking you're a jerk, that she hates you, or that you're just so mean! With empathizing through mirroring, however, she'll walk away thinking, *Hmm, maybe Mom has a point* or *Wow! I can't believe I just said that to my mom.* You want her to reflect on her own behavior, not yours. I know this advice is counterintuitive. Your brain will be telling you, *I have to let her know this isn't okay.* But trust me, she already knows it isn't okay. That's why she did it in the first place! Yelling or fighting back only frays the bond more and perpetuates the conflict.

What if my spouse/partner won't do it? Will it still work?
It may take a bit longer, but it will work. What usually happens is that the child becomes more attached to and compliant with the parent who is mirroring. And when the other parent realizes the technique is working, he buys into the program as well. That doesn't always happen; you may always be the only one doing it, but that's okay too. You'll be giving your teen that important emotional nutrition that builds emotional resilience so that she can cope with whatever the other parent does or says. And in situations where parents are divorced, the home of the one who is mirroring tends to become a kind of oasis of safety for the teen.

How am I going to find the time to do all this mirroring? I've got enough to do already.
You don't have the time *not* to do it. Mirroring and connecting take less energy and are more effective than nagging, yelling, and

bribing. The difference is that, when you mirror, you put more of that energy into the beginning of the conversation. When you fight, more energy is expended as the conflict escalates. What's more, if you employ the technique on a regular basis, you'll have less corrective or de-escalating mirroring to do over time. You get a really good return on your initial time investment.

I can't believe my kid is really going to go for that baby stuff. What do I do if he rejects it?

If your teen doesn't want you near him, if he jerks away from you every time you make an overture, just take it slow. Look for those little connecting moments. Eventually there'll be one time when he doesn't jerk away, or he lets you sit next to him for a few minutes. You can't get defensive about this. If he does reject you, just say okay, you know I love you and I'm here. Don't look defeated, injured, or wounded. That will only make things worse. Eventually he'll come around.

If you're really disconnected, leave a note or a baby picture or some other token on his pillow. And don't talk about it!

How do I mirror when my kids are fighting with one another?

I hear this a lot. You have to separate them. Go to the more compliant one first, and do your mirroring: "I really want to know what's going on here. I want to make sure I get it right, and it's very confusing. So do me a favor and think about what I need to know." Make sure you get the urgency you're feeling into your voice when you do this. Then, when he's gone off to think, address your other child: "Okay, now tell me what happened." Make sure you echo back exactly what he says. As you do this, you'll often find that he starts to self-correct: "Well ... maybe it wasn't exactly ... I might have ..." Then you can agree on a consequence if necessary. If there's restitution to be made, try to decide together what it should be. Or, you can leave him to think about it while you go back to the first kid and repeat the process.

If they won't separate, you can mirror to each one in front of the other. "So, he's saying … and you're telling me that it didn't happen that way at all …" In effect, you're becoming a family therapist, making each kid feel that you're listening to him. You do a lot of reframing by repeating back what they're saying without actually agreeing or disagreeing with either one of them. Ultimately you want to do what Alyson Schafer, in her book *Honey, I Wrecked the Kids*, calls putting them in the same boat so that they can figure out together how they're going to stay afloat. If they can't or won't do that, you may need to intervene and impose a consequence.

If I do all this mirroring with one of my kids, isn't that unfair to the others?

Well, yes it would be. You need to mirror with all your kids, whether or not they have behavioral issues. Everyone's brain needs this emotional reinforcement. There can be other benefits, too. For example, when a child sees you mirroring with her more troublesome sibling, she might just step back and think, *Mom handled that very well. Maybe she'll handle things better with me, too.* By listening well, and neither over- nor underreacting, you'll establish a track record and earn the trust of all your kids.

I did all this mirroring and our relationship improved, but now it has deteriorated again. What do I do now?

Most people remember to mirror when their kid is behaving badly, but then, when things improve, they get complacent and forget the incidental mirroring, which is the glue that holds it all together. So the behavior sneaks back, and when you notice it, you feel exhausted. You might have thought you'd be better able to handle the behavior after a respite, but exactly the opposite happens. You think, *Oh no, I can't go through this again!* Once you've had a taste of the good life the last thing you want is a return to the bad old days.

You need to go back to square one, but understand it won't take very long—usually no more than a day or two—to get back to where you were. Mirroring and connecting need to be a way of life, not a stopgap.

My difficult kid is much, much better, but now my "good" kid is starting to act out. What do I do now?
This all goes back to the interdependent nature of the family dynamic. If something changes within that dynamic, it's bound to change something else. If the child who was always in trouble is no longer in trouble, the good one loses his self-definition. *If I'm not the good one, then who am I?* That can be quite upsetting for a child, so he'll start to test the waters, and may try out different tactics to discover his new place in the family system. Or perhaps you haven't been mirroring and connecting so much with your easier child because you've been so focused on the difficult one. If that's the case, increasing your mirroring and setting more limits will very quickly get him or her back on track. Finally, it may be that the "good" kid isn't really acting any differently, but that you're now noticing behaviors you'd formerly been willing to overlook.

Just be aware that this can happen so that it doesn't throw you for a loop. Use the same techniques with this child as you did with the other, and you'll be fine.

What if I really don't want to do it?
If you really don't want to, you probably really need to. I tell my clients to adopt the CALM technique not just for their kids but for themselves, because ultimately it's going to make their lives easier. If you can't do it in the moment when you're really angry,

concentrate on the incidental mirroring you do when things are going well. Either way, this is something your teen needs. If he needed medicine or an operation you'd do everything in your power to get him what he needed, and he needs this just as much. Remember, too, the child you least feel like doing this with is the one who needs it the most.

Isn't it manipulative to use this technique on your teen?
If you're doing it to manipulate him, then it's manipulative. If you're not honestly empathic but are doing it to shut your kid up or get him to behave, he'll sense that and it won't work. Mirroring and connecting have to begin from a place of love.

Connecting for a
Lifetime and Beyond

You're about to go out and try this on your own—although I hope you'll return to this book as you work to master the CALM technique. Before you put the book down, I'd like to offer a few final words of caution and encouragement.

First, keep in mind that the tools I've been giving you are not a short-term cure. Practicing connected parenting isn't like taking an antibiotic for ten days with the expectation that when you stop your infection will be gone. If you stop, all the difficulties you were having will return.

As I constantly remind the parents with whom I work, once you begin to CALM your teen, she'll begin to behave better. At which point, I can almost guarantee, you will begin to relax. You'll mirror less frequently and you'll probably forget to look for those all-important connecting moments. And then your teen will start to act out again.

When that happens, you'll be surprised by how quickly the old behaviors return and how intensely you react. You might think that because the relationship grew closer and the behavior disappeared for a time, you'll be better able to cope with the relapse. The exact opposite is almost always true.

Over and over parents tell me that their teen talked back to them or threw a fit over something trivial, and they, the parents, panicked. Having had a taste of the good and peaceful life, they couldn't imagine having to deal once more with the trouble they experienced in the past.

Monitor your teen's behavior. If it's deteriorating, you need to tighten the rope and rev up your mirroring, because your teen has temporarily lost that sense that you have his back. He's testing you to find out just how far you're going to let him fall. His behavior is a kind of communication that will let you know how he's feeling. Things will get better, then worse, then better again. The more you CALM and connect, the quicker the right tension will be restored.

You may need to remind yourself how far you've come. Parents who see their children every day sometimes don't notice how much they've changed until their little boy is shaving or their little girl brings home her first steady boyfriend. The same is true of behavioral change. Try to notice those changes: *Wow, Jeff actually gave me a hug today. Emma didn't throw a fit when I told her that her favorite sweater was at the cleaners!* You might consider keeping a journal to help you track the changes. Discuss what you've noticed with your spouse or partner. There may be some troublesome behaviors that want to stick around, but even those will emerge less frequently and with decreasing intensity. You'll enjoy longer periods when things go smoothly.

Many parents notice that their teens start to cry more frequently. Kids often use anger and sullenness to mask sadness. When they feel safe they're able to cry more easily. So tears can mean that the connection between you is strong enough for your teen to let you know how he really feels. If that happens, by continuing to mirror you'll be demonstrating that it's okay to cry and that you're strong enough to tolerate his sadness. Eventually you'll find that your teen no longer needs to use behavior to show you what's wrong. Because you've proved to be a good listener, he'll be able to tell you with words.

While all this is still a bit new, you may be unconsciously waiting for the other shoe to drop, anticipating that phone call from school or waiting for the next door slam. It can take a few months to accept that the changes really have taken hold. In addition, now that things seem so much better, you may notice all the little things you'd let slide because you were dealing with the big issues. And then, of course, there may be a sibling—the so-called "easier" child—who suddenly decides it's her turn to act out. This happens more often than you'd imagine. But you now know why, and you also know what to do.

Above all, remember that teens *will* act out and behave badly from time to time. It's their job! What matters is how you react. I can't promise to give you a perfect child, but the techniques I teach will help you deal more positively when she's a little less than perfect.

Parenting is probably the hardest job anyone can ever have, but it's also the most important and rewarding. By the time your child is a teenager, you have only a few more years before he goes off to be an adult. And so I urge you to ask yourself these questions: *What do I want my children to remember about their teen years? What will I feel when my teenager is gone and I look back on myself as a parent? What do I want my teen to remember about me?*

We all want our kids to remember how deeply loved and understood they felt. That gift will last them a lifetime. And it's a gift they can pass on to their own children.

Suggested Reading

Amen, Daniel G. *Change Your Brain, Change Your Life*. New York: Three Rivers Press, 1999.

Bradley, Michael J. *Yes, Your Teen Is Crazy!* Gig Harbor, WA: Harbor Press, Inc., 2003.

Childre, Doc Lew and Howard Martin. *The Heartmath Solution*. New York: HarperOne, 1999.

Clavier, Dr. Ron. *Teen Brain, Teen Mind*. Toronto: Key Porter, 2009.

Coloroso, Barbara. *The Bully, the Bullied, and the Bystander*. New York: Harper Paperbacks, 2009.

———. *Just Because It's Not Wrong Doesn't Make it Right*. New York: Penguin Global, 2008.

Dispenza, Joe. *Evolve Your Brain*. Deerfield Beach, FL: Health Communications, Inc., 2008.

Doidge, Norman. *The Brain That Changes Itself*. New York: Penguin, 2007.

Epstein, Robert. *The Case Against Adolescence*. Sanger, CA: Quill Driver Books, 2007.

Glasser, Howard, and Jennifer Easley. *Transforming the Difficult Child*. Tuscon, AZ: Nurtured Heart Publications, 1999.

Gordon, Karyn. *Dr. Karyn's Guide to the Teen Years*. New York: Collins, 2008.

Green, Ross W. *Lost at School*. New York: Scribner, 2008.

Gurian, Michael. *The Purpose of Boys*. San Francisco: Jossey-Bass, 2010.

Kendall, Philip C. *Child and Adolescent Therapy*. New York: Guilford Press, 2005.

Kutscher, Martin L. *Kids in the Syndrome Mix*. London: Jessica Kingsley, 2007.

Levin, Diane E. and Jean Kilbourne. *So Sexy So Soon*. New York: Ballantine, 2009.

Mamen, Maggie. *The Pampered Child Syndrome*. London: Jessica Kingsley, 2005.

Maté, Gabor. *In the Realm of Hungry Ghosts*. Berkeley, CA: North Atlantic Books, 2010.

———. *Scattered*. New York: Plume, 2000.

———. *When the Body Says No*. Hoboken, NJ: Wiley, 2011.

Neufeld, Gordon and Gabor Maté. *Hold On to Your Kids*. New York: Ballantine, 2006.

Schafer, Alyson. *Honey, I Wrecked the Kids*. Hoboken, NJ: Wiley, 2009.

Siegel, Daniel J. *The Developing Mind*. New York: Guilford Press, 2001.

Wiseman, Rosalind. *Queen Bees and Wannabes*. New York: Three Rivers Press, 2009.

Acknowledgments

To all the people who have attended my workshops and courses, thank you so very much. I would thank each one of you individually if I could. Your passion, your love for your children, and your support for Connected Parenting have inspired me and kept me moving forward.

To all my clients past and present, thank you for inviting me into your lives, for letting me get to know you and your wonderful children. You inspire me every day with your courage, honesty, and devotion to your kids, and you make me love my job.

To my agent, Rick Broadhead, thank you so much for believing in this project, for your ongoing support, and for your belief in Connected Parenting.

To Jonathan Webb, my editor at Penguin Canada, thank you so much for getting behind this book and helping me to clarify my important message.

Judy Kern, you are amazing. Thank you for all your help with this book. I may even send you a copy of this one. You're brilliant, funny, and on my list of favorite people. I am so grateful for everything you've done. I'll miss talking to you every week. It almost makes me want to write another book ... almost.

Faye Mishna, your wisdom, your teaching, and your wonderful clinical skills are what have inspired Connected Parenting, and I am forever grateful.

Robin Stone, you are such a good friend. You hold me up whenever I feel like giving up, and you make me a better person. Thank you for your contribution to Connected Parenting and to the website. Your essays are so inspirational, so funny, so wise, and so important. Thank you. Lunch? But I may have to cancel.

Alisa Kenny-Bridgeman, thank you for all your support, for reading my manuscript, and for all your input over the years. You are an amazing friend, psychologist, and mother, and I'm lucky to know you! Maybe you and I will even get over our imposter syndrome one day.

Cindy Smolkin, my good friend and right-hand man. You are so good at what you do. I cannot express how lucky I feel to have you beside me on this journey. Your exceptional skills, your beautiful way with families, and your wicked sense of humor make you an absolute treasure. I'm so excited to be in this with you; the journey has just begun.

Janis Beach, thank you for your wisdom, your steady and intelligent manner, and your ability to see the big picture. You are incredible and such a gifted therapist. I still pinch myself every day that you're part of the Connected Parenting management power team. I cannot thank you enough, and I'm so looking forward to discovering where we go next. Onward and upward!

Lisa Seward and Barb Miller, members of my dream team, thank you for everything you do for Connected Parenting, for your experience, passion, and wisdom. I'm so very lucky and so honored that you've chosen to work with me. I can't wait to see where it all goes from here.

Bev Kavanagh, thank you for your belief in me and my work and for your beautiful and caring heart. You have no idea how much I'm inspired by your unending love for your son and your constant ability to see the best in people.

Sarah Hall from Bluesky Communications, you've been so wonderful to work with. Always there when I need you and so on top of things. Thank you for all your hard work.

Audrey Grushcow, you're one of the smartest people I know. I'm so grateful for all the work you did for me on my website and for your passionate belief in Connected Parenting.

Kim Schewitz, thank you for your help in getting me focused, for helping me to understand my worth, and for helping me learn to have more confidence in the business side of things. You taught me a lot and I'm so thankful.

Gabor Maté, thank you for your belief in Connected Parenting, for the support you've given me, and for helping me to believe in the power and importance this message has for all the parents out there. We are all better because of your inspirational work.

Dr. Till Davy, you are one of the biggest reasons why Connected Parenting thrives! Thank you for all of your referrals, for your passion, for your support and belief in Connected Parenting. You are extraordinary at what you do, and I am grateful beyond words.

Jackie Brown-Hart, keep it fresh! Thanks for our endless talks about this book and your help with titles. Now what? Thank you for making Quinn Lake (my happy place) an even happier place for me.

Jenny Hall, thank you for your support, for our great talks, and for being such an important part of Quinn Lake for me. See you at the beach, hopefully before three p.m.

Kim Pitters, thanks to you, John, Holly, and Tori for being a wonderful family. I love you all.

Max: Thanks Max. You may not realize it, but you helped me a great deal. You are a great kid. Keep believing in yourself. Thanks for keeping me up to date on all the latest technology.

Quinn Lake teens: Thanks for your wisdom and insight. Thank you for sharing your opinions and for helping me catch a glimpse of what it's like to be a teen. It was too long ago for me to remember.

Scott Lindsay, Uncle Dog, you are the best. Thanks for stepping up and taking over the website. You are seriously smart. I love you.

Neola Husbands-Kolari, I'm so happy that you're part of this family, I love you! I'm so happy that the funny little girl I met so long ago is a part of my life every day. It is a privilege to watch you grow up.

Alyson Schafer, it has been so wonderful getting to know you. I think you're fantastic. It's so nice to have your support and to be able to talk with someone who has the same unusual life.

Joey Shulman, my twin separated at birth, thanks for all the morning breakfasts and listening to me whine. I love that we get each other. Thanks for being you.

Jacqueline Green, thank you for reaching out to me. It has been a pleasure getting to know you and working with you. I'm looking forward to future collaborations.

Tish Cohen, this is a hard one. How do you capture in a few lines what you need to say to your best friend? Especially when I just wasted a whole line saying that. I love that we've had one running conversation since we were twelve years old. I love that we haven't really matured all that much. You are my friend, my Houston. Together we are one person.

My kids, Jacob, Zoë, and Olivia, words cannot explain how much I love you all. You are my life and I'm grateful for you every minute of every single day. Thank you for being so understanding when I get busy and for being exactly who you are.

Mom and Dad, the best parents in the world, you really are Connected Parents. You're so special and show your unconditional love to me every single day. I love you both more than you will ever know.

Rebecca Lindsay, my sister, my rock, you keep Connected Parenting running. You have endless patience for me and share my passion for this work. I said it in my last book but I need to say it again: It makes me sad for all the people who don't know what it's like to have a sister.

Barry, my husband, my love, you know how much I love you and how happy I am to be traveling through this wonderful life with you. You make every day warm and wonderful. Thank you for supporting me, for being proud of me, and for mirroring even when I know you're doing it. You're the best husband anyone could ever ask for. Thank you.

Index